Natural Sweets
and
Healthy Treats

NATURAL MEALS PUBLISHING
for Better Health the *Natural* way

ISBN 1-882314-16-6
96 pp. $7.95

Published by Natural Meals Publishing
Website: www.naturalmeals.com
Email: order@naturalmeals.com
Order/Fax Line: 888.232.6706

Illustrations by Clair Bingham
Cover photo by Kimberly Bingham
Cover design by Ginni LeVar

FOREWORD

Food! Food!! Food!!! Everywhere, food! If that is what we can call it! In the dictionary food is defined as *"any substance that can be metabolized by an organism to give energy and build tissue."* Yet, as you will discover in what you are about to read, this is not what is happening with the food our youth, and our population in general, are consuming. Instead of building up and regenerating our bodies, what we are eating is tearing down our bodies. We live on party food and snacks, on the run, everyday. And our choices are killing us. Literally!

We live in a world where eating on the run has become a way of life, and snacks are the *main menu*! We just *love* TREATS. But let's take a look at those treats - there's nothing in most of them that will serve to build a healthy body! A toaster pastry and soda on the way to school, a coffee and donut on the way to work, a mid-morning bag of chips or a chocolate bar and soda as a pick-me-up that leaves us dragging an hour later, burger and fries inhaled as we grab lunch on the run to our next commitment, soda and candy bar to get us through the afternoon. Then we pick up KFC or pizza at the drive through on the way home because we're just too pooped to prepare dinner when we get there!

Finally, we plunk ourselves in front of the TV or computer after gobbling down the pizza or chicken, and probably another soda, and of course, inspired by all of the TV commercials for fast food treats, we munch away on chips and dip, or cookies and hot chocolate until we fall into bed, completely spent. Not spent from a healthy game of tennis or an evening walk in the neighborhood with the family. Simply from eating foods that have no nutritional value to speak of and which do not have the capacity to replenish the energy that we have spent trying to get through our day.

In my work with family nutrition and lifestyle, I see so many young people suffering with illnesses that were once considered adult onset maladies, such as type 2 diabetes, hypertension, heart disease, and various forms of cancer - not to mention obesity at younger and younger ages. Without a doubt we are facing a health crisis as never before seen in humanity.

Degenerative diseases, the result of poor nutrition and lifestyle choices, will result in a generation of children born since the year 2000 living shorter life spans than their parents unless we make some serious changes in what we put in our stomachs and how we physically use our bodies NOW!

It would be unrealistic to think that we will stop eating on the run any time soon. Or that we will stop eating snack foods and treats. So the trick is to *make the snack foods count for something, from a nutritional standpoint,* and to teach people how to make the healthier selections on a regular basis so that the food we eat does what it is supposed to do - give energy and build tissue. There is no one I know of who is better equipped to assist us on that journey to healthier treats than Rita Bingham, the author of several incredibly healthy, wholesome recipe books. This book is filled with valuable information about the health concerns facing all of us today, as well as some of the most tasty solutions to our cravings for sweets and other snack foods. They are simple and easy to prepare, and sinfully delicious. The best part is that *you don't have to feel guilty when you eat them!*

Dr. Marilyn Joyce, RD
Author of **"5 Minutes To Health"** & **"I Can't Believe It's Tofu!"**

TABLE OF CONTENTS

Introduction 6

Glossary 18

All Things Cool...21
    Smoothies and Cold Drinks 22
    Flavored Water...28
    Easy Frozen Treats..29
    Ice Cream 33
    Sherbet..35
    Cashew Creams 37

Candies...41

Cookies, Bars, and Muffins 49
    No-Bake Cookies 50
    Baked Cookies...53
    Bars..58
    Life On The Go Bars...58
    Muffins 69

Crispy Crunchies.......................................71
    Savory Crunchables...72
    Sweet Crunchables 77

Dips...81
    Savory Dips 82
    Sweet Dips 86

Snack Wraps..89

Index 94

Books to Add to Your Library 96

INTRODUCTION

In our other books, we've supplied healthful whole food recipes for every meal of the day, but very few recipes for snacks or desserts, because we believe that the **best** snacks are raw fruits and vegetables. But since so many people **are** snacking these days, and since there's such an influx of UN-healthy products being touted as "good for you", we decided the time had come to supply you with nutritious, delicious alternatives.

Caution!! Most of these recipes are treats, and most treats should be consumed occasionally, rather than every day. Don't get caught in the trap of thinking that if a recipe is made with healthful ingredients, you can eat as much as you want and still be healthy. Eating too much fat, too much sugar, or too many carbohydrates (whether they're refined or not) creates an unhealthy body. Balance is the key.

THE PROBLEM

We are a nation of snackers and most of us feel the need to indulge ourselves often. We most often choose quick meals (either from a can, a box, or from a fast-food restaurant) and tasty snacks that are loaded with fats and sugars. There's nothing wrong with fast meals and snacks that taste good, but most of us choose our snacks based on TASTE alone, rather than on how those foods will affect our health.

These poor decisions can take a toll on our health. It's up to us to "take charge of our health" and start feeding our bodies what they need to help reverse some of these startling statistics:

- **BREAST CANCER** According to the National Cancer Institute, based on current rates, 13.2 percent of women born today will be diagnosed with breast cancer at some time in their lives.
- **ESOPHAGEAL CANCER** According to the American Cancer Society, over the past 25 years, the incidence rates of esophageal cancer have risen by more than 570 percent, clearly following the rise in intake of carbonated soft drinks.
- **HIGH CHOLESTEROL** American Heart Association statistics state that half of all Americans age 20 and older have cholesterol levels that are 200 or higher. (The good news is, you can make many lifestyle changes to lower your cholesterol and reduce your risk of heart disease and stroke.)

- **OBESITY** The American Obesity Association figures show that the number of adults who are overweight or obese has continued to increase (despite the millions of dollars spent on diets, exercise equipment, diet pills, etc.). Currently, 64.5 percent of U.S. adults, age 20 years and older, are overweight and 30.5 percent are obese.
- **ARTHRITIS** According to the Center of Disease Control, arthritis is the leading cause of disability in the United States, with: 9,500 deaths, 750,000 hospitalizations, and 51 billion in medical costs.
- **DIABETES** National Diabetes Statistics show 10.9 million men and 9.7 million women aged 20 years or older have diabetes, with complications such as, heart disease and stroke, high blood pressure, kidney disease, and periodontal disease. Dr. Steven Aldana, author of "**The Culprit & The Cure**", writes that 91% of diabetes cases are avoidable!

ARE THESE JUST "ADULT" DISEASES? NO! OUR CHILDREN'S HEALTH IS ALSO DECLINING:

- **OBESITY** The American Academy of Child & Adolescent Psychiatry statistics show that between 16 and 33 percent of children and adolescents are obese, and that unhealthy weight gain due to poor diet and lack of exercise is responsible for over 300,000 deaths each year. The complications of obesity are increased risk of heart disease, high blood pressure, and diabetes.
- **CORONARY ARTERY DISEASE** A 25 year study in Bogalusa, Louisiana, conducted on children eating a typical American diet, showed that fatty deposits appear in the coronary arteries by age 3, increasing to 70 percent by age 12. These fatty deposits represent early stages of coronary artery disease.
- **CANCER** According to the UCSF Children's Hospital statistics, cancer kills more children than any other disease. Each year, about 2,300 children and teenagers die from cancer, and about 11,000 more children are diagnosed with it.
- **ADHD** The Centers for Disease Control and Prevention (CDC) found that 7% of children 6-11 have been diagnosed with ADHD.

PAYING THE PRICE

My grandchildren are the 4th generation to live with an abundance of "fast food". Many Americans truly believed they could eat whatever they wanted, and their doctors could keep them "healthy". **It's NOT working!** We're now seeing the results of living on "manufactured" refined food. Most snacks and sweet treats are loaded with white flour, white sugar, hydrogenated oils (trans fats) and chemicals that wreak havoc with the body's natural balance. **In short, they destroy health.**

CRITICAL STATE OF CHILDREN'S HEALTH

David L. Katz. M.D., Director of the Yale University-Griffin Hospital Prevention Research Center, warned in the March 10, 2004 *Wall Street Journal*, **"There shouldn't be a parent in the U.S. who has not heard…our children are projected to have a shorter life expectancy than their parents. Children are being more harmed by poor diet than by exposure to alcohol, drugs and tobacco combined."**

HOW DID WE ARRIVE AT THIS CRITICAL STATE?

Rather than giving our children the "gift of health", too many of us are just giving in to their wants by allowing them to have too many treats, too many sweets, too many refined foods, and way too MUCH food! Our children are usually eating what we're eating, so our health is also deteriorating at an alarming rate.

FOOD CHOICES

FOOD CHOICES AFFECT HEALTH

We want the BEST health, but we often make the WORST choices for our health.

Too many TREATS – not enough nutrient-dense calories.

Too many SWEETS – too many high-sugar and high-fat snacks in place of regular, balanced meals (It is now estimated that children consume ¾ CUP of sugar every day! That's over 5 pounds a week! The RDA for sugar is 0!! It's time to get the sugar OUT.)

Too many BAD FATS – margarine, and the hydrogenated oils that make foods shelf-stable.

Too many REFINED FOODS – candy, sodas, chips, fries, burgers, and white breads/pastries. Dr. William Sears calls carbonated drinks "diabetes in a bottle". REFINED CARBOHYDRATES are the problem – not the carbohydrates that occur naturally in whole foods.

Not enough GOOD food – whole grains and beans, fresh, ripe, **RAW** fruits and **RAW** vegetables.

TOO MUCH FOOD – The body can only process about 500 calories at a time into fuel; the rest is stored as fat.

SNACK FOODS REPLACE MEALS

A few years ago, it was estimated that Americans eat an average of 23 pounds of processed snack food products each year. That's only one OUNCE a day! If you've looked recently at the contents of many shopping carts going through the check-out line in your grocery store, it's easy to see that the "average" person eats *much* more "junk" than that, when you consider fries, chips, candy, donuts, and other desserts that are eaten at, or instead of, meals. We believe the figure is now much closer to one POUND a day.

Rather than having an *occasional* treat, we now want tasty snacks and decadent desserts at ANY time of the day or night. With our "on the go" lifestyle, we've come to rely on snack foods to sustain us, rather than eating most of our food at regular mealtimes. What we choose to eat is based first on TASTE, then on CONVENIENCE, and if HEALTH is considered at all, it's usually always dead last on the list of considerations. This is one of the major reasons for our increased rate of disease, not to mention our flabbier, heavier bodies.

ORGANIC JUNK FOOD

Everything in a *health store* is supposed to be HEALTHFUL. Right? With the advent of the "health food store" many people have switched from highly processed Twinkies®, Ding Dongs® and Snickers® to *Organic* Energy Bars, *Organic* Potato Chips, and *Organic* Chocolate Chip Cookies – most of which are merely Organic Junk Food. If you check the labels, you'll find that most of what you're buying is still made with white sugar (even if it was made from organically grown cane!); many of the popular potato chips are fried in hydrogenated oil; and most of the cookies are made with white or unbleached flour (even if it was made with organically grown wheat!). And, you're paying "top dollar" for this Organic Junk Food!!! Just because you're shopping at a *health food* store doesn't mean you're always getting the most *healthful* foods.

Fat is still fat, whether you're eating chips fried in partially hydrogenated oils, or organically grown and minimally processed or unrefined oils. They are still fried (it's just too tempting to eat more than the body can handle), and still un-healthful.

Calories are still calories, regardless of the source, and if you eat more calories than your body needs, you're going to gain weight. Yes, it's better to "upgrade" your sugars, fats, breads, pastas, etc., but if the balance is wrong and you're regularly choosing too many high-fat or high-sugar snacks, rather than eating mostly fruits and vegetables for your meals and snacks, your body is going to suffer because of that imbalance.

Sugar is still sugar, whether it is in the form of honey, refined white sugar, or even our favorite - Sucanat. Any of these can still cause an imbalance in blood sugar, as well as weight gain from the extra calories.

One Year No-Sugar Challenge

In an effort to help our teenage daughter lose weight and make better food choices, we told her we'd pay her to cut out refined sugar for 1 year, because we knew that refined sugar causes cravings and makes weight loss hard, if not impossible.

Things went well for a while, and then she started substituting health food store treats made without refined sugars, but didn't cut down on the *number* of treats she had. Needless to say, she stopped losing weight. Were the sugar cravings still there? No, but she still ate more because the unrefined or less-refined sugars were considered "legal".

After the year, when she started eating "normally" again, she gained all her weight back, and then some, because she hadn't learned to choose healthier snacks or to limit quantities.

The bottom line? No good habits were formed, so no permanent improvements were made. From this experiment, we learned that sweets of any kind can entice us to overeat, and that balance is crucial. If we want the *best* health possible, then the food we put into our bodies should be fresh picked, and vine-ripened - as close as possible to the way God created it.

Portion Size Grows Bigger

We've chosen Big, BIGGER, BIGGEST in our serving sizes, especially at fast food restaurants, not to mention the all-you-can-eat buffets! Even at home, we have larger meals on much larger plates than ever before. We have also super-sized our sweet treats: huge muffins, huge cookies, huge ice cream cones and sundaes, and oh my, those *huge* sodas! Consequently, we now consume far more calories (most of them severely lacking in or devoid of nutrients) than our bodies require or can utilize, resulting in the staggering statistics showing that nearly 2 of every 3 Americans are overweight or obese.

TAKING ACTION

THINK OF SNACKS AS "MINI-MEALS"

Choose from foods that will nourish the body with the vitamins, minerals, antioxidants, fiber, proteins and healthful unsaturated fats necessary to function properly. (Obviously, it makes sense to not have unhealthful foods readily available to them.)

When children are consistently offered nutritious foods, their tastes change and they begin to make better choices on their own. When we eat more nutritious food, we crave more of the same!! I am constantly amazed when this phenomenon occurs!

Many of my clients report that, after several months on Juice Plus+®, and without making any other dietary changes, they, their children, *and* their husbands have begun making healthier meal choices! What an incredibly easy way to improve nutrition and get on the "road to better health"!

BUY AND SERVE THE BEST SNACKS (NATURE-MADE)

"HEALTHFUL" snacks are...
1) Full of FIBER – soluble and/or insoluble, found in whole grains, fruits, and vegetables
2) Loaded with Phytochemicals – "plant" chemicals that provide all the nutrients necessary to fight disease
3) Rich in naturally-occurring vitamins and minerals, in the proper balance, just as God created them
4) Low in fat, salt, and sugar (unrefined, of course).

Choose from:
>   Fruits and Vegetables – raw
>   Fruit Smoothies
>   Veggie Trays and Dips (skip the chips)
>   Nuts and Seeds – raw
>   Popcorn (air-popped and then seasoned with sea salt, olive oil, Butter Buds®, Season-All®, or a little real butter)

ELIMINATE THE WORST SNACKS (MAN-MADE)

Snacks to ELIMINATE are made of...

1) Refined flour
2) Refined sugar
3) Refined fats (margarine, shortening, hydrogenated or partially hydrogenated oils)
4) MSG, in any of its many forms
5) Artificial anything (color, flavor, etc.)

LIMIT OR ELIMINATE MILK AND DAIRY PRODUCTS

Many children drink milk as a snack. With all the recent information about hormones and antibiotics used in raising and maintaining cows for milk and meat production and the detrimental effects this is having on children and adults, it makes sense to look at alternative milks from the plant kingdom.

In my book, "**1-2-3 Smoothies**", you'll find 3-minute recipes for many different types of non-dairy milk, including our favorites: oat, rice, and barley.

What? No cheese? We've tried some excellent cheeses made from almond, soy and rice milks. They're surprisingly good. Did you know that most low-fat and fat-free cottage cheese, yogurt, and sour cream contain "artificial color" and that this "color" is usually titanium dioxide, the pigment used in white paint? Yikes!

AVOID THE FOLLOWING:

Soda Pop and Sports Drinks, including ALL diet drinks
French Fries
Donuts
Chips (potato or corn, unless baked without fat)
Candy Bars
Pork Rinds
Cookies/Cakes/Pastries - fat-free are the worst because they pretend to be healthful.
Crackers – look for trans-fats on the list of ingredients
Pretzels – most are made with refined flour. Just because it doesn't have sugar doesn't mean it's healthful!
Ice Cream
Popsicles (unless made from 100% fruit juice)

According to Dr. William Sears, "If you're eating food from a package and you didn't package it, it's probably 'junk food'."

DRINK MORE WATER!

Make sure to drink water often (and please, filter out the chlorine!). Our bodies need lots of pure water (half of our body weight in ounces of water). Water makes everything in our bodies work better, especially the brain.

When we feel "hungry" for a snack, it's often the body's way of asking for more water. Once the body is well hydrated, these "hungries" most often disappear.

WISDOM BRAND'S SWEETLEAF® FLAVORED STEVIA

If you're not used to drinking plain water, try adding a few drops of Wisdom Brand's SweetLeaf® Flavored Stevia to each cup of water. Our favorite flavors are Root Beer, Chocolate Raspberry, English Toffee, Vanilla, Orange, Lemon, Grape, Dark Chocolate, and Peppermint.

To order online, go to www.naturalmeals.com/stevia.

READ THE LABEL

If you're going to BUY commercially-prepared snacks, you'll need to educate yourself. If the list of ingredients is long and filled with unpronounceable words, you can bet that product is not FOOD, and truly is not something that should be inside YOUR body.

I looked up some commercial food additives, their purpose, and the problems they can cause. The ones I found most interesting are:

Glutamic Acid – Alzheimer's

Phosphoric Acid – (found in soda pop) loss of bone calcium

Sodium Diphosphates – Alzheimer's and osteoporosis trigger

Sodium Sulphite – asthma trigger

Sulphur Dioxide – interferes with absorption of nutrients, damage to DNA, cardiovascular conditions and asthma.
(www.additive-free.co.uk/e_numbers.htm)

Dr. David Katz, medical contributor for ABC News and nutrition columnist for The Oprah Magazine, recommends that we turn our children into "Nutrition Detectives" and search for the harmful ingredients on the labels of foods they like to eat. Then, educate them about the reasons why these foods are damaging, rather that healthful.

Additives and Preservatives to Avoid:

According to Jayne Benkendorf, author of the OSAAT® Rebel, "Additives and preservatives are used in our food for two primary reasons. First, as a **preservative:** Preservatives are used to keep foods from spoiling and to increase the shelf life of food – in the grocery store as well as our pantries. Second, as an **additive:** Additives are added to food primarily to make it look and/or taste better.

"For example, artificial colors may be added to make a product more appealing to children, and artificial flavors are used to produce a particular taste that manufacturers believe will help sell their product. Most highly processed foods would be almost tasteless without these added flavors. And of course, artificial additives and preservatives are very inexpensive compared to the 'real' thing.

"The following additives and preservatives, in my opinion, pose some very serious health concerns especially when consumed on a regular basis:

Artificial flavors (benzaldehyde, methyl salicylates, and 1,500 others)
Artificial colors (Red #40, Red #3, Citrus red #2, Yellow #5, Yellow #6, Blue #2, etc.)
Aspartame (NutraSweet®/Equal®)
Sulfites (sulfur dioxide, potassium bisulfite, sodium bisulfite, sodium sulfite, potassium metabisulfite, sodium metabisulfite)
Nitrates & Nitrites"

Rebel – Additives & Preservatives, January, 2005. For more information, contact Jayne Benkendorf at jayne@osaat.com.

Avoid Trans Fat

What is trans fat? Basically, trans fat is made when manufacturers add hydrogen to vegetable oil—a process called hydrogenation, which increases the shelf life and flavor stability of foods containing these fats.

Trans fat can be found in vegetable shortenings, most margarines, crackers, cookies, snack foods, and other foods made with or fried in partially hydrogenated oils. Unlike other fats, the majority of trans fat is formed when food manufacturers turn liquid oils into solid fats such as shortening and margarine. (FDA Consumer Magazine, Pub No. FDA04-1329C)

WHAT'S WRONG WITH TRANS FAT?

Trans fat is in virtually all packaged foods, and now there's evidence showing they lower *good* cholesterol and raise *bad* cholesterol levels. (Henderson, K Study, "Stealth Fat Lurks in Favorite Foods" 2003)

Research shows that animals eating processed, high fat foods for only 8 weeks were unable to perform simple memory tasks as well as those on a high fat diet of soybean oil. (MUSC study, 3/11/2004)

According to an excellent article on fats written by Mike Furci, consumption of Trans Fats:

Increases arterial inflammation

Promotes improper management of blood sugar (of special importance to diabetics)

Interferes with the function of the immune system

Decreases the body's ability to utilize omega-3 fatty acids

Decreases the amount of healthy omega-3 fatty acids in our tissues
(www.bullz-eye.com/furci/2006/fats_lipid_hypothesis.htm)

Dr. Katz says the *recommended level of trans fat intake is ZERO*. (Check out Dr. Katz' website www.thewaytoeat.net for information on making healthful choices.) So, where are the trans fats in *your* cupboard? Yes, we know they are in all the foods that taste SO good, but are you willing to risk the damage they cause?

THE TOP 10 "TRANS FAT" FOODS:

1. **Packaged foods.** Cake mixes, Bisquick™, and other dry mixes of this type all have several grams of trans fat per serving.

2. **Fast food.** Fries, chicken, and other foods are almost always deep-fried in partially hydrogenated oil. Even if the restaurants use liquid oil, fries are sometimes partially fried in trans fat before they're even shipped to the restaurant.

3. **Baked goods.** Even worse news—more trans fats are used in commercially baked products than any other foods, including donuts, cookies, cakes, cream-filled cookies, etc.

4. **Chips and crackers.** Shortening provides a crispy texture. Even "reduced fat" brands can still have trans fat. Anything fried such as potato chips, corn chips, cheese curls, etc., contains trans fat.

5. **Frozen foods.** Frozen pies, pot pies, waffles, pizzas, and breaded fish sticks. Even if the label says it's "low-fat", if there's oil listed on the label, you can be sure it still contains trans fat.

6. **Cookies and candy.** Check out the label. What is the serving size? If you chow down on a few handfuls of those, you've eaten a *lot* of trans fat.

7. **Breakfast food.** Breakfast cereal, granola bars and energy bars.

8. **Soups.** Ramen noodles and soup cups.

9. **Toppings and dips.** Non-dairy creamers and flavored coffees, whipped toppings, bean dips, gravy mixes, and salad dressings.

10. **Spreads.** Margarine and other non-butter spreads and shortening are loaded with trans fats and saturated fats, both of which can lead to heart disease.

Watch out for labels that say "0 grams trans fat" because this usually just means that if you eat a *very* small serving size, you'll get less than 1/2 gram of trans fat. If the label has partially hydrogenated oil on it you can be sure you *are* eating trans fats.

Can you eliminate trans fat *entirely* from your diet? Only if you never eat commercially prepared foods – but you CAN offer healthier alternatives and reduce the exposure to these damaging fats, while reducing your risk of heart disease.

CHOOSE THE BEST INGREDIENTS

When purchasing grains, sweeteners, or oils, choose those with the least amount of refining and the fewest additives.

Bad	Better	Best
Enriched White Flour	Unbleached Flour	100% Stone Ground Whole Wheat (or gluten-free) Flour
White Cane Sugar	Organic Cane Sugar	Jaggery, Sucanat, Demarara, Rapadura, Honey, Molasses, Stevia

Artificial Sweeteners	Organic Cane Sugar	Jaggery, Sucanat, Demarara, Rapadura, Honey, Molasses, Stevia
Hydrogenated Oil	Olive or Canola Oil	Unrefined or Cold-Pressed Oils – Olive, Walnut, Canola, Grapeseed
Margarine	Butter	Butter Blend (1/2 Olive or Grapeseed oil, and 1/2 Butter)

THE BOTTOM LINE

PREVENTION IS THE KEY

Since over 75% of all deaths are diet- and lifestyle-related (www.nutritionstreet.com), it's up to each of us to make all the changes we can to reduce our risk of disease, instead of waiting until we have a degenerative condition. Proper nutrition is important for everyone, but once we lose our health, it's hard to get 100% of it back.

So, my advice is to eat more whole foods! Eat more raw foods because they're loaded with phytonutrients and enzymes. Get back to the basics. Eat foods as close to "fresh picked" as possible!!!

Arm yourself with information - go to www.naturalmeals.com and sign up for our free monthly e-newsletter, Nutri-News. We'll provide you with the latest information on the power of whole foods for better health.

For those who don't, won't, or can't eat enough fresh, ripe, raw fruits and vegetables every day, I recommend **Juice Plus+**®, which is primarily fruits and vegetables in capsule, chewable or gummi form. It's not a substitute for fruits and vegetables, but it can help bridge the gap between what we *should* eat, and what we *do* eat.

Juice Plus+® is the only supplement we take, and the only one I recommend. It is the most well-researched nutraceutical in the world. For more information, visit www.juiceplus.com.

GLOSSARY

Barley Flour - Made from whole barley, this flour can be added to wheat flour to increase fiber as well as vitamins and minerals.

Barley Malt Powder - A natural sweetener derived from an extract of sprouted barley. As a sugar substitute, Barley Malt is a natural whole food and is less likely to cause blood sugar highs and lows. Most brands contain about 10% maltodextrin (from corn) to limit clumping and allow for free flowing. Maltodextrin is a pure carbohydrate that is a complementary sweetener.

Bean Flours (white bean, garbanzo bean, etc.) - Beans ground to a flour cook in only 3-5 minutes and make nutritious, delicious soups and dips! They can be purchased in many grocery stores and most health food stores. Or, grind your own at home using a wheat mill (see *Whole Wheat Flour* in this section).

Black Raspberry Powder - Nutri Fruit™ Black Raspberry Freeze-Dried Powder is 100% pure freeze-dried black raspberries and can be ordered at www.nutri-fruit.com or by calling 1-866-343-7848.

Bragg Liquid Aminos - Similar to tamari soy sauce, but not fermented or heated.

Caraway Seeds - Crescent-shaped seeds with an anise-like flavor that are most often used as a spice in breads, especially rye bread.

Chocolate Chips - Those made with evaporated cane juice are a little healthier version than traditional chips made with refined sugar and milk. We found that Tropical Source® had the best flavor. They melt easily and are vegan.

Cocoa / Carob Powder - We use Wonderslim® brand cocoa powder because it is decaffeinated. If you'd rather not use cocoa, use carob powder. We prefer a mixture of 1/2 carob powder and 1/2 cocoa powder.

Coconut Milk - A mildly sweet, milky white cream pressed from the meat of a mature coconut. It is high in fat, but a good substitute for dairy milk in some recipes.

Evaporated Cane Juice or Demarara - More refined than Sucanat, but far less than white sugar. Golden tan color, which is lighter than Sucanat, but less molasses-like in flavor. Florida Crystals® and Wholesome Sweeteners® brands can be found at health food stores and some grocery stores.

Flax Seeds - To ensure freshness, grind your own flax seeds to a fine meal, using an ordinary seed or coffee mill. In mine, I grind flax, sesame, sunflower, all types of nuts, as well as small amounts of wheat or rice for breakfast cereals, sandwich fillings, salads, or pilaf. Golden flax seeds are picked before maturity, so we prefer the "vine ripened" dark seeds.

Garam Masala - A blend of spices common in Indian food. Each brand has a different flavor, so it might be best to buy several brands and see which one you like best.

Guar Gum / Ultra Gel® / Xanthan Gum - Thickening agents made from plants. These products are great for thickening liquids such as salad dressings, dips, gravies, and sauces. Xanthan gum is often used as a substitute for gluten in yeast breads and other baking. These products are usually available in health food stores. Note: Saliva breaks down the thickening agent in these products, so don't take a taste from your mixing spoon and then put it back into the mixture!

Jaggery - The traditional unrefined sugar of India. It is much like honey or maple syrup that has turned sugary. Although the word is used for the products of both sugar cane and the date palm tree, technically, jaggery refers solely to sugar made from sugarcane. Best of all, the process does not involve chemical agents. The one drawback is that Jaggery comes in a "lump". Look for a fairly soft "lump"!

Juice Plus+ Complete® - A whole food based beverage product offering balanced nutrition in every scoop. It's great-tasting, all-natural, non-dairy, and contains Juice Plus+® fruit and vegetable powders, along with a proprietary blend of other foods and nutrients typically lacking in today's diet. It has NO dairy, NO fast-releasing or artificial sugar, and is made entirely from plant sources. It contains all the basic nutrients required for a balanced meal. Juice Plus+ Complete® comes in two delicious flavors: French Vanilla and Dutch Chocolate. When used in our "On The Go Bars", you create a snack that satisfies longer.

Juice Plus+ Thins® - Chewable, fiber-containing wafers that may help curb hunger. Juice Plus+ Thins® do not contain any stimulants. Juice Plus+ Thins® contain a powerful combination of natural ingredients including: fruit powders and extracts; AbsorbaLean™, a carefully balanced blend of soluble and insoluble dietary fibers; a special plant-based blend of nutritional chromium; natural, slow-release sweeteners including Fruit Source® grape juice solids. Thins® come in two great flavors: Chocolate Fudge and Apple Cinnamon.

Lime Oil - An essential oil derived from the skin of the citrus fruit. It can be purchased online or in a health food store.

Maple Syrup - Use the "real thing", Grade A Dark Amber, 100% Pure Maple Syrup, rather than imitation syrup, which contains corn syrup, high fructose corn syrup, water, cellulose gum, and a host of other artificial flavors and preservatives.

Natural Peanut Butter - Buy all natural - just peanuts and salt. We like Adams®, Smucker's® and Peanut Butter & Co® (go to www.ilovepeanutbutter.com to find a store in your area that sells this brand. It comes in white chocolate, dark chocolate and cinnamon raisin, and is sweetened with cane juice instead of refined sugar). In many health food stores, "grind your own peanut butter" machines can be found in the bulk section, allowing you to choose salted or plain.

Nut, Grain, or Seed Milks - Almonds, cashews, brown rice, oats, barley, quinoa, and sesame seeds make excellent milk alternatives, without cholesterol or lactose. Buy unfortified, organic, unsweetened milks, or make your own. See **"1-2-3 Smoothies"** by Rita Bingham for easy 3-minute plant milk recipes.

Powdered Milk / Dry Milk Powder - Made from cow's milk. Most health food stores sell dry milk powder in bulk. If milk is grainy, not powdered, blend to a fine powder before measuring. Also available as a non-dairy substitute is Better Than Milk® Soy or Rice Milk Powder.

Sesame Tahini - A paste made from ground sesame seeds. It is a major ingredient in hummus and other dishes from the Middle East. It can be purchased at most health food stores.

Soymilk - A milk-like drink derived from soybeans. The liquid is produced by soaking soybeans and grinding them with water. Soymilk is ideal for people with lactose intolerance or milk allergies; it also contains polyunsaturated and monounsaturated fats that are good for the heart. The best choice for soymilk is one that is unsweetened, unfortified, and organic. Choose brands that are full-fat. If you want to reduce the fat content, just add a little water! We like WestSoy® organic, unsweetened, and unfortified. It's shelf-stable, so we keep a case in the pantry.

Stevia - An herb native to Paraguay that is several hundred times sweeter than table sugar and virtually calorie-free. It is labeled a "dietary supplement" by the FDA and sold in health food stores in powder or liquid form. Stevia rates as a zero on the glycemic index, which ranks foods on how they affect our blood sugar levels. We use it to sweeten our smoothies, muffins, uncooked candies, and to flavor our water. For more information about Stevia, visit http://www.naturalmeals.com/stevia.

Sucanat (or SUgar CAne NATural) - Juice pressed from the sugar cane, concentrated into a thick syrup, dehydrated, and then milled into a grainy substance, without refining or adding chemicals.

Tamari - A wheat free soy sauce popular with those who have wheat allergies.

Vanilla Extract - Most vanilla extracts contain sweeteners, including high fructose corn syrup. We now use only Vanilla Creme Stevia or organic vanillas that do not contain sugar or additives of any kind. Our favorites are Vanilla de Tahiti®, http://vanillafromtahiti.stores.yahoo.net/vanillaextract.html, and Nielsen-Massey Organic vanillas. We now use less, and enjoy recipes more! For your convenience, the vanilla extract used in these recipes is the "normal" kind. If you use an unsweetened brand, adjust recipes accordingly.

Whole Wheat Flour - In recipes calling for whole wheat flour, freshly ground tastes and works best! We grind our own and most often use Hard White Wheat. This wheat is lighter in color than Hard Winter Wheat (usually called Turkey Red Wheat), but still very nutritious. Two popular grain grinders are the K-TEC Kitchen Mill and the WonderMill (previously WhisperMill). Both of these mills will also grind legumes.

ALL THINGS COOL

Cold drinks and frozen desserts are popular at any time of the year, but there's nothing like fresh, vine-ripened fruits to add a unique burst of flavor.

These homemade treats, made with natural ingredients, not only taste great, but they will actually nourish rather than damage the body, so try them all...but not too often!

For those who avoid dairy, you'll love our "nut milk" desserts!

Smoothies and Cold Drinks

The best choice for soymilk is one that is unsweetened, unfortified, and organic. Choose brands that are full fat. If you want to reduce the fat content, just add a little water.

Depending on the strength of your brand of vanilla extract, you may want to add more or less than the recipe calls for.

Vanilla Nut Shake

1/4-1/2 c. cold water
1 c. soymilk
1 c. crushed ice
1/2 banana
2 T. natural peanut butter
1/4 c. (1 scoop) Juice Plus+ Vanilla Complete®

Blend all ingredients until smooth.

Banana Maple Smoothie

1 c. soymilk
1 banana
2 T. maple syrup
2 t. vanilla extract
1/4 c. (1 scoop) Juice Plus+ Vanilla Complete®
9 ice cubes
Optional: 2 T. ground flax

Blend all ingredients until smooth.

Banana-Ade

2 ripe bananas
2 c. orange juice or 1/2 c. orange juice concentrate and 1 1/2 c. water
5-6 fresh or canned pineapple chunks

Combine all ingredients in a blender and blend until smooth.

EMILEE'S BANANA FREEZE

3 frozen bananas*
2 c. soymilk
2 t. vanilla extract
3-4 T. honey
15-20 ice cubes
1/8 t. nutmeg

Blend all ingredients until smooth.
Variations:
Vanilla 'Nana Freeze – Add 1/4 c. (1 scoop) Juice Plus+ Vanilla Complete®.
Banana Popsicles – increase honey to 1/3 c. and pour into popsicle molds or cups. Freeze until solid.

*Buy a big bunch of bananas, and allow them to ripen. Then, peel bananas and place in a zip-top bag in the freezer.

VERY BERRY BANANA SMOOTHIE

1 1/2 frozen bananas
3/4 c. frozen blackberries
1 c. frozen strawberries
2 c. water
2 t. vanilla extract
1/4 c. Old Orchard® 100% Apple Raspberry Concentrate
1/4 c. (1 scoop) Juice Plus+ Vanilla Complete®

Blend all ingredients until smooth and creamy.

PEACH DREAM

4 c. frozen peaches or 3 fresh peaches
1 c. soymilk
1 frozen banana
3 T. honey*
2 t. vanilla extract
1/4 c. (1 scoop) Juice Plus+ Vanilla Complete®

Combine all ingredients in blender and blend until smooth and creamy.

*Reduce honey if using very sweet peaches (vine-ripened).

BLUEBERRY BOOST

1 c. soymilk
1 frozen banana
1 c. blueberries, fresh or frozen
1/4 c. (1 scoop) Juice Plus+ Vanilla Complete®
2 T. 100% White Grape Juice Concentrate
2 t. vanilla extract
8 ice cubes

Combine all ingredients in blender and blend until smooth and creamy.

TROPICAL TREAT SMOOTHIE

1/2 c. coconut milk
1/2 c. soymilk
1 c. crushed pineapple
1 1/2 frozen bananas
2 t. vanilla extract
1 T. honey
1/4 c. (1 scoop) Juice Plus+ Vanilla Complete®
2 t. lime juice

Combine all ingredients in blender and blend until smooth and creamy.

RAZ-A-MANGO SMOOTHIE

2 c. soymilk
1/4 c. (1 scoop) Juice Plus+ Vanilla Complete®
2 t. vanilla extract
1 frozen banana
1 1/2 c. frozen mango chunks
1 c. frozen raspberries
2-3 T. Welch's® 100% White Grape Raspberry Concentrate

Blend all ingredients until smooth.

Raz-a-Nana Smoothie

1 1/2 c. frozen raspberries
1 1/2 frozen bananas
1 c. soy or rice milk
2 T. honey
2 t. vanilla extract
1/4 c. (1 scoop) Juice Plus+ Vanilla Complete®

Combine all ingredients in blender and blend until smooth and creamy.

Soy-Orange Julius

1 c. soymilk
1/4 c. 100% orange juice concentrate
1/4 c. (1 scoop) Juice Plus+ Vanilla Complete®
1 frozen banana
2 t. vanilla extract

Combine all ingredients in blender and blend until smooth and creamy.

Shannon's "Drinky Drink"

1 12 oz. can 100% White Grape Juice Concentrate*
1 12 oz. can water
Juice of 2 limes or 1 lemon**
6-8 fresh mint leaves
Approximately 24 ice cubes

Combine all but mint leaves in blender and blend until ice is completely smooth. Add the mint leaves last and blend until they are reduced to tiny specks. Serve immediately.

*Be sure to get the 100% juice variety of juice concentrate. The "juice drink" and "100% juice" labels look very much the same.
**You can use lemon juice in place of limes, but I found that the lime juice brings out the taste of the mint and makes the drink taste much better.

BERRY TASTY "DRINKY DRINK"

1 12 oz. can Welch's® 100% White Grape Raspberry Concentrate
1 12 oz. can water
Juice of 2 limes
10 fresh mint leaves
Approximately 24 ice cubes
1/2 c. fresh or frozen raspberries (opt.)

Combine all but mint leaves in blender and blend until ice is completely smooth. Add the mint leaves last and blend until they are reduced to tiny specks. Serve immediately.

STRAWBERRY MINT BREEZE

1/3 c. Welch's® Strawberry Breeze Juice Concentrate
4 frozen strawberries
1 T. honey
3-4 ice cubes
1 c. water
6 large mint leaves

Blend all ingredients until smooth.

STRAWBERRY PUNCH

1 c. fresh or frozen strawberries
1 1/2 c. soymilk
2 T. honey
2 T. frozen orange juice concentrate
1 t. vanilla extract

Combine all ingredients in blender and blend until smooth.

Soy Nog

6 c. soymilk
1/4 t. nutmeg
1 t. vanilla extract
1 t. imitation rum extract
3/4-1 c. Sucanat or dried cane juice

Blend all ingredients and serve chilled.

Honey Soy Nog

4 c. soymilk
1/4 t. nutmeg
1 t. vanilla extract
1 1/2 t. imitation rum extract
1/3 c. honey
1 t. guar gum (optional - for thickening)

Blend all ingredients and serve chilled.

Soy Egg Nog

This is a delightfully believable egg nog substitute, although it does contain artificial flavoring. We only serve this at Christmas!

6 c. soymilk
2 eggs
3/4-1 c. Sucanat or dried cane juice
1/4 t. nutmeg
1 t. vanilla extract
1 t. imitation rum extract

In a medium saucepan over medium-high heat, bring 2 c. of the soymilk to a slow boil. Place eggs in blender; add 1/2 c. of the hot soymilk and blend. Pour into saucepan, while stirring. Reduce heat to medium; add Sucanat or dried cane juice and nutmeg and cook 2 minutes. Add vanilla and rum extract. Serve chilled.

A TASTY WAY TO DRINK MORE WATER

We find that it's easier for everyone, especially children, to drink more water if it *tastes* good. Commercially prepared flavored waters are loaded with artificial flavorings and sweeteners. You can make your own tasty grape drink by adding about 2 T. 100% purple grape juice concentrate to 2 cups water. Squeeze a slice of lemon into the glass and you have a thirst-quenching treat.

Or, try Wisdom Brand's SweetLeaf® Flavored Stevia. At the time of this printing, there are twelve flavors and we like them all! For more information or to order, visit www.naturalmeals.com/stevia.

LEMON GRAPEADE

2 c. water
1 T. fresh lemon juice
10 drops SweetLeaf® Grape Liquid Stevia

Place all ingredients in a glass, stir and drink! Add ice, if desired.

FLAVORED WATERS

Root Beer – 1 cup water plus 8 drops SweetLeaf® Root Beer Liquid Stevia

Lemon Drop – 1 cup water plus 7 drops SweetLeaf® Lemon Drop Liquid Stevia

Grape – 1 cup water plus 7 drops SweetLeaf® Grape Liquid Stevia

Orange Julius – 1 cup water plus 7 drops SweetLeaf® Valencia Orange Liquid Stevia and 2 drops SweetLeaf® Vanilla Crème Liquid Stevia

Chocolate Raspberry – 1 cup water plus 8 drops SweetLeaf® Chocolate Raspberry Liquid Stevia

Chocolate Toffee – 1 cup water plus 7 drops SweetLeaf® Milk Chocolate Liquid Stevia and 3 drops SweetLeaf® English Toffee Liquid Stevia

Chocolate Mint – 1 cup water plus 7 drops SweetLeaf® Dark Chocolate Liquid Stevia and 4 drops SweetLeaf® Peppermint Liquid Stevia

Chocolate Cinnamon – 1 cup water plus 6 drops SweetLeaf® Dark Chocolate Liquid Stevia and 6 drops SweetLeaf® Cinnamon Liquid Stevia

Raspberry-Mint Flavored Water

2 quarts water
1/4 c. 100% White Grape Raspberry Concentrate
1 1/2 t. lime juice
8 mint leaves, chopped

Combine all ingredients in a 2-quart container and stir well. Leave mixture in the fridge for an hour or so to chill and allow flavors to combine. Strain out mint leaves before serving.

Easy Frozen Treats

Frozen Fruit

A delightful treat for hot summer days is fresh frozen fruit. Grapes, cherries, and bananas make great frozen snacks. I like them so much that I eat them in the winter too! I wrap myself in a blanket and sit in front of the fireplace! Wash fruit (except bananas), take off stems and place in a zip-top freezer bag. You can pit the cherries if you want, but it is not necessary. Freeze several hours or until firm.

Banana Freezies

1 banana

Cut banana into 1/2" slices. These slices can be frozen and eaten plain, rolled in raw or roasted chopped nuts (pecans, walnuts, almonds, peanuts), dipped in chocolate dipping sauce (recipe follows), or dipped in chocolate AND rolled in nuts (this is my personal favorite!). Coconut or granola are also great toppings. If you are going to coat these slices with one of the above, slice the banana, roll in your choice of nuts, coconut or granola, then freeze until firm.

CHOCOLATE DIPPING SAUCE FOR BANANA FREEZIES

1/2 c. carob or chocolate chips
2 t. soymilk
1 t. butter

Combine all ingredients in a small saucepan on medium heat. Stir constantly; reduce heat if necessary to prevent burning. Stir until chips are completely melted and ingredients are well mixed. Remove from heat. With a toothpick, spear banana and coat with chocolate sauce. If desired, roll in chopped, roasted nuts. Place on a lightly oiled plate and freeze for several hours.

CHILLY HAYSTACKS

1/2 c. honey
1 T. olive oil or butter
1/2 c. natural chunky peanut butter
2 t. vanilla extract
1 c. unsweetened coconut

Boil honey and oil to soft ball stage. Add remaining ingredients and chill in refrigerator until mixture forms a "haystack" when dropped from a spoon. Store in refrigerator.
Kid-pleasing variation: If you want to turn your "haystacks" into "dirt clods", roll in chopped, roasted, salted nuts while still warm.

B'NANA-NUT SQUARES

1 banana
1/4 c. (1 scoop) Juice Plus+ Vanilla Complete®
1 1/2 T. natural chunky peanut butter
1/2 c. chopped raw walnuts

Combine everything except walnuts in a food processor and process until smooth, about 1 minute. Sprinkle 1/4 c. walnuts in bottom of 8" square pan and pour mixture into it, topping with remaining 1/4 c. walnuts. Freeze until solid. Cut into squares and serve.

CHOCO-'NANA-NUT POPS

1 banana
1/4 c. (1 scoop) Juice Plus+ Chocolate Complete®
1 1/2 T. natural chunky peanut butter

Mash the banana and stir in other ingredients. Spoon into popsicle molds and freeze until solid.
Variation: Omit the peanut butter and add 4-6 drops of SweetLeaf® Chocolate Raspberry Liquid Stevia. Coat with chopped, roasted, salted nuts.

CITRUS MINT POPSICLES

2 c. water
3/4 c. 100% orange juice concentrate
4 T. lime juice
1 T. lemon juice
3 T. evaporated cane juice or honey
8 mint leaves

Blend all ingredients except mint leaves until smooth. Add mint leaves and pulse until leaves are reduced to tiny specks. Pour into popsicle molds or cups and freeze until solid.

LEMON GRAPE POPS

3 c. water
2 T. lemon juice
48 drops SweetLeaf® Grape Liquid Stevia

Combine ingredients, pour into popsicle molds, and freeze for several hours. It tastes pretty good for being mostly water!!!

Note: 40 drops = 1/2 t.

CHOCOLATE MINT POPS

3 c. soymilk
2 t. carob or Wonderslim® cocoa powder
36 drops SweetLeaf® Dark Chocolate Liquid Stevia
54 drops SweetLeaf® Peppermint Liquid Stevia

Place ingredients in blender jar and blend until smooth. Pour into popsicle molds and freeze until solid.

Note: 40 drops = 1/2 t.

PUMPKIN PIE COOLERS

1/2 c. canned pumpkin
1/2 c. evaporated milk or concentrated rice milk*
1 t. molasses
3 T. honey
1/4 t. cinnamon
1/8 t. each nutmeg and cloves
A few sprinkles of ginger (or 1/16 t.)

Blend all ingredients until smooth. Pour into popsicle molds or 3-oz paper or plastic cups and freeze for several hours until solid.
*Using Better Than Milk Rice Milk Powder, use only 1/2 the water called for to reconstitute.

ORANGE CREME POPS

3/4 c. orange juice concentrate
1/2 c. organic whipping cream
1 c. peach or orange yogurt (sweetened with fruit juice, not sugar)
1/2 c. evaporated cane juice
1 1/2 c. soymilk

Combine ingredients in blender, except whipping cream, and mix well. Add whipping cream and pulse to mix. Pour into popsicle molds and freeze until firm.

ICE CREAM

Although there are very specific descriptions of ice cream and sherbet, we are classifying our recipes in the following way:

Ice Cream - contains organic whipping cream for an extra smooth, creamy texture and taste. (While we usually avoid dairy products, these "occasional treat" ice creams are the exception, because they're SO good! We use very little in each recipe, but it makes a *big* difference.)

Sherbet - may contain soymilk or coconut milk to add smoothness and texture while enhancing the great fruity flavors.

MANGO ICE CREAM

3/4-1 c. 100% White Grape Juice Concentrate*
2 c. soymilk
1 large mango, peeled and seeded
1/2 c. water
1/2 c. organic whipping cream
2 t. vanilla extract

Blend all ingredients except whipping cream, then add and pulse just to mix (mixing too much makes butter!). Pour into ice cream maker and follow manufacturer's instructions.

*If you like sweeter ice cream, use 1 c. white grape juice concentrate. Remember, the frozen product always tastes less sweet.

RASPBERRY MANGO ICE CREAM

1 12 oz. can Old Orchard® 100% Apple Raspberry Concentrate
3 c. soymilk
1 1/2 c. fresh or frozen mango chunks
2 t. vanilla extract
1/2 c. organic whipping cream

Blend all ingredients except whipping cream, then add and pulse just to mix (mixing too much makes butter!). Pour into ice cream maker and follow manufacturer's instructions. Makes 6 cups before freezing.

WATERMELON ICE CREAM

4 c. blended watermelon (use seedless, or just strain out the seeds after blending)
3/4 c. evaporated cane juice
1/2 c. soymilk
2 t. vanilla extract
1/2 c. organic whipping cream

Combine and pour into ice cream maker and process until very thick. For a firmer ice cream, transfer from freezer bowl to serving dish and freeze 4-6 hours.

CHOCOLATE ICE CREAM

2 1/2 c. soymilk
2 c. water
1 1/2 c. evaporated cane juice
1 c. Wonderslim® cocoa powder
2 t. vanilla extract
1/2 c. organic whipping cream

Combine water and evaporated cane juice in a saucepan and place over medium heat, stirring until crystals dissolve. Whisk in cocoa and simmer for 3 minutes, stirring constantly. Remove from heat and refrigerate mixture until completely cooled. Stir in soymilk, cream and vanilla; pour into ice cream maker, then follow manufacturer's instructions. The ice cream is done when it is fairly thick (kind of like soft-serve), but if you like firmer ice cream, transfer from freezer bowl to serving dish and freeze 4-6 hours.

Variation: **Nutty Chocolate Ice Cream** – add 1/2 c. raw chopped pecans, walnuts, or almonds to the machine when ice cream is semi-frozen and allow machine to mix in the nuts.

SHERBET

TROPICAL TRIO SHERBET

1 c. fresh or frozen mango chunks
2 c. coconut milk
1 c. water
1/2 c. 100% White Grape Juice Concentrate*
1 c. crushed pineapple

Blend all ingredients except pineapple until smooth. Stir in crushed pineapple, and pour into ice cream maker and follow manufacturer's instructions. Makes 5 1/2 cups.

*Depending upon the sweetness of the mango, you may need to increase white grape juice concentrate to 1 c.

LEMON SHERBET

2 1/4 c. water
1 c. evaporated cane juice
2 T. lemon zest, finely grated
2/3 c. fresh lemon juice
1/4 c. soymilk

Combine evaporated cane juice and water in a saucepan and boil rapidly for 30 seconds. Add lemon juice and zest, then put mixture in refrigerator until completely cool. Add soymilk, then pour mixture into ice cream maker. Process until very thick. Serve as is, or freeze for several hours.

Soy-Orange Sherbet

3 c. soymilk
1 c. plain yogurt
1 c. orange juice concentrate
1/4 c. honey
3/4 c. Sucanat
2 t. vanilla extract

Blend until very smooth. Place in ice cream freezer bowl and process until very thick. For a firmer sherbet, transfer from freezer bowl to serving dish and freeze 4-6 hours.

Coco-Mango-'Nana Sherbet

1 ripe banana
2 mangoes, peeled and seeded
1 c. coconut milk
1/2 c. water
1/2 c. evaporated cane juice
2 t. vanilla extract

Combine ingredients in blender jar and blend until smooth and creamy. Pour into ice cream maker and follow manufacturer's instructions.

"Just Peachy" Sherbet

1/3 c. raw cashews
3 ripe peaches
1 c. coconut milk
1 c. water
3/4 c. light honey
2 t. vanilla extract

Blend until very smooth. Pour into ice cream freezer bowl and process until very thick. For chunky sherbet, add a diced peach near the end of processing time. For a firmer sherbet, transfer from freezer bowl to serving dish and freeze 4-6 hours.

CASHEW CREAMS

Cashews and other nuts make "milk" when blended with water. They make an excellent base for these creamy frozen desserts.

CHOCOLATE CASHEW CREAM

1 1/2 c. raw cashews
1 c. cold water
1 c. ice and enough water to measure 1 cup
1 c. Sucanat
2 t. vanilla extract
1/3 c. Wonderslim® cocoa powder

Combine ingredients in blender and blend until smooth and creamy. Pour into ice cream maker and follow manufacturer's instructions.

Variations:

Chocolate Mint Cashew Cream – add 2-3 drops peppermint extract to the mixture.

Double Chocolate Nut Cashew Cream – add 1/2 c. chopped carob or chocolate chips and 1/2 c. chopped, toasted almonds near the end of processing time.

RASPBERRY CASHEW CREAM

3/4 c. raw cashews
1 c. ice and enough water to measure 1 cup
1/2-3/4 c. fruit sweetened raspberry jam
1/4 c. pure maple syrup (or evaporated cane juice)
1/3 c. chopped, toasted almonds (opt.)
1/2 t. vanilla extract

Combine all ingredients except almonds, if used, and blend until smooth. Stir in almonds and pour into ice cream maker and follow manufacturer's instructions.

Variation: **Raspberry Chip Cashew Cream** – add 1/4 c. chopped carob or chocolate chips to mixture after blending.

CLAIR'S FAVORITE STRAWBERRY CASHEW CREAM

1/2 c. raw cashews
1 c. ice and enough water to measure 1 cup
1 1/2 cans Welch's® Strawberry Raspberry Concentrate
1 can coconut milk
3/4 c. Sucanat
1 t. vanilla extract
2-3 drops natural red food coloring (opt.)

Combine ingredients in blender and blend until smooth and creamy. Pour into ice cream maker and follow manufacturer's instructions.

BLUEBERRY CASHEW CREAM

1 frozen banana
1 c. frozen blueberries
3/4 c. Sucanat
1 1/2 c. raw cashews
1 c. cold water
1 c. ice and enough water to fill the measuring cup
2 t. vanilla extract

Combine all ingredients and blend until smooth. Pour into ice cream maker and follow manufacturer's instructions. Makes 4 cups liquid.

PEANUT BUTTER-BANANA CASHEW CREAM

1 1/2 c. raw cashews
1 frozen banana
1 c. water
1 c. crushed ice
1/4 c. natural peanut butter
1 t. vanilla extract
3/4 c. Sucanat
1/2 c. carob or chocolate chips, chopped (opt.)
1/2 c. toasted peanuts, chopped (opt.)

Combine all ingredients except chips and peanuts, if used, and blend until smooth. Add chips and nuts, pour into ice cream maker and follow manufacturer's instructions.

Coconut Cashew Cream

1/2 c. jaggery or Sucanat
1 c. water
1 c. raw cashews
1 c. crushed ice
1/2 c. coconut milk

Combine jaggery and water in a bowl and let sit for 10 minutes to soften. Place all ingredients in blender and blend until smooth. Pour into ice cream maker and follow manufacturer's instructions. Makes 3 cups liquid.

Variation: **Vanilla Nut Cashew Cream** – add 1 1/2 t. vanilla and 1/2 c. chopped toasted almonds to mixture after blending.

Choco-Peanut Cashew Cream

1 1/2 c. raw cashews
1 c. ice and enough water to measure 1 cup
1 c. cold water
1 c. Sucanat
1/4 c. carob or Wonderslim® cocoa powder
1 t. vanilla extract
1/2 c. natural crunchy peanut butter

Blend nuts, ice, and water until smooth. Add all but peanut butter and blend again. Add peanut butter and pulse just to mix in. Pour into ice cream maker and follow manufacturer's instructions. Makes 3 1/2 cups liquid.

Watermelon Sorbet
Incredibly easy to make, and oh, SO delicious!

3 c. blended watermelon (seedless, or strain out seeds after blending)
1/2 c. raw cashews
1/2 c. demerara cane sugar

Blend 1 c. of watermelon juice with remaining ingredients until very smooth. Add remaining juice and pour into ice cream freezer bowl and follow manufacturer's instructions. Makes 3 3/4 c. liquid.

BANANA CASHEW CREAM

2 c. soymilk
1 c. cashews
1 frozen banana
1/2 c. evaporated cane juice
8 ice cubes
1/2 c. raw walnuts, chopped (opt.)

Blend all ingredients except nuts until very smooth. Chill mixture in the refrigerator for about an hour and then transfer to ice cream maker and follow manufacturer's instructions. Add nuts at the last (if used), giving them just enough time to mix in. Makes 4 c. liquid.

MAPLE NUT CASHEW CREAM

1 1/2 c. raw cashews
1 c. cold water
1 c. ice and enough water to fill the measuring cup
3/4 c. maple syrup
2 t. vanilla extract
1/3 c. walnuts, chopped

Combine all ingredients except walnuts and blend until very smooth. Chill for about an hour in the refrigerator. Pour into ice cream maker and follow manufacturer's instructions, adding walnuts at the very last.

"BROWN SUGAR" BANANA CASHEW CREAM

1 c. raw cashews
2 c. soymilk
3/4 c. Sucanat
1 t. vanilla extract
3 1/2 c. ice and enough water to measure 1 cup
1 banana

Blend first four ingredients until very smooth. Add remaining ingredients and blend until smooth. Chill in the refrigerator for about an hour and then transfer to ice cream maker and follow manufacturer's instructions. Makes 4 c. liquid.

CANDIES

With so many commercial candies on the market, these family favorites have been all but forgotten. Bring the children and grandchildren into the kitchen with you and make these candies together. They'll love being able to make a treat that's actually GOOD for them! Some can even be made without supervision, so turn them loose and see how creative they become.

These tasty candies are easy to make, require very few ingredients, and very little time and effort. What could be better?

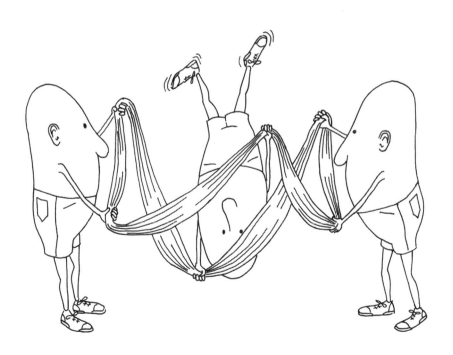

HONEY CANDY

This tasty candy can be made with dairy, soy, or rice milk powders)

1 1/2 c. dry milk powder
1 T. butter
1/2 c. honey, warmed
1 t. vanilla extract

Stir and knead enough dry milk into honey to make a firm ball. (The amount of dry milk powder needed depends on the temperature and water content of the honey.) Stretch and form into rolls that are pencil thin. Let stand for 3-4 hours. If rolls flatten out, gather up and work in more dry milk powder. Roll out again and cut into bite size pieces.

Variations:
Add carob or chocolate chips, coconut, granola, or your favorite crunchy cold cereal.

Berry Candy - Add 1 1/2 T. Nutri Fruit™ freeze-dried black raspberry powder. (See p. 18 for ordering information.)

Pink Peppermint Candy - Omit vanilla from Basic Candy and add 1 1/2 t. peppermint flavoring and 2-3 drops natural* red food coloring (or a few drops of beet juice).

Orange Candy - Omit vanilla and add 1 1/2 t. orange extract and a drop or two each natural* yellow and red food coloring.

Lemon Candy - Omit vanilla and add 1 1/2 t. lemon extract and a few drops of natural* yellow food coloring.

Peanut Butter Candy - Omit butter and add 1/2 c. natural crunchy or smooth peanut butter. This candy is great served cold. For variety, I put it in the freezer after rolling, and when I want a tasty treat, I just break off a chunk!

Nut 'n Honey Candy - Add 1 c. finely chopped almonds (raw or toasted).

*Natural food colors are made from real *food*. Check out your local health store, or visit this interesting website for sources: http://www.neelikon.com/natcol.htm

Peanut Butter and Jelly Barber Poles

1 recipe Honey Candy with Berry Candy Variation
1 recipe Honey Candy with Peanut Butter Candy Variation

Roll each recipe into pencil-sized rolls and let stand to dry slightly. Cut into 10" pieces, pinch together on one end, and twist the two flavors into "barber poles". Lay on a plate and allow to air-dry 3-4 hours. Cut into bite-sized pieces.

Nut Rolls

1 recipe Honey Candy
3/4 c. ground walnuts

Spread Honey Candy out thin on a surface coated with dry milk powder to prevent sticking. Use a rolling pin if necessary. Sprinkle with the nuts and press into mixture. Roll up like a cinnamon roll, then cut slices about 1/2" thick with dental floss (slip floss under roll and cross to cut). Let dry slightly or sprinkle with powdered Sucanat to remove any stickiness.
Variations: Turn other variations of Basic Honey Candy into nut rolls by adding nuts. Orange Nut Rolls are really tasty!

Honey Caramels

2 c. honey
1 c. evaporated milk or concentrated rice milk*
1 T. vanilla extract
3 T. butter
1/16 t. sea salt
1 c. raw walnuts, chopped

Mix honey and milk together and cook, stirring constantly to prevent burning, to firm ball stage, about 245° F. Stir in vanilla, butter, salt, and nuts. Pour into a lightly buttered cake pan or onto a plate and let cool. Cut into squares, or roll into balls and wrap in waxed paper.
*Using Better Than Milk® Rice Milk Powder, use only 1/2 the water called for to reconstitute.

MOLASSES TAFFY

1 c. honey
1 c. mild molasses
1/2 c. water
1 t. vanilla extract
2 T. butter
1/4 t. baking soda
Sprinkle of sea salt

Mix honey, molasses and water in a saucepan and boil to soft crack stage, about 275-285° F. Remove from heat and stir in remaining ingredients. Pour onto a lightly buttered plate, let cool enough to handle, then stretch. If after 2 minutes of stretching the taffy does not form a firm rope, getting lighter in color as you work more air into it, then it has not been cooked long enough. Return to saucepan and cook longer. Lay stretched taffy out in rope shape. Break into pieces by hitting sharply with a knife handle.

Variation: **Molasses Caramels** - mix in 1 c. chopped walnuts and stretch for about 5 minutes to give it a chance to cool and firm up a little. Roll into balls or logs and wrap in waxed paper. If mixture is too sticky to do this, put a *little* bit of butter or oil on hands and keep stretching. Too much oil will cause mixture to lose its stiffness.

CHOCOLATE LOGS

1 c. honey
1/4 c. carob or Wonderslim® cocoa powder
1/4 c. carob or chocolate chips
1 c. dry milk powder
2 t. vanilla extract

Cook honey to hard ball stage, about 260° F. Remove from heat and add chips and vanilla, stirring until melted. Whisk in cocoa powder and dry milk (make sure there are no dry milk chunks!). Pour onto a lightly buttered plate and let cool enough to handle. Form rolls to the thickness of a pencil, cut into 2 inch "logs" and wrap in waxed paper.

CHOCOLATE MINT HONEY CANDY

1/2 c. honey
5 drops mint extract
1 T. carob or Wonderslim® cocoa powder
1 1/2 c. dry milk powder

Boil honey for 30 seconds in a small saucepan, then remove from heat and add mint and cocoa powder. Stir well. Gradually stir in dry milk. You may want to take mixture out of the saucepan and knead it on a covered plate or countertop sprinkled with dry milk power. Roll into pencil-thin logs and cut into bite-sized pieces.

CAROB CHIPPERS

1/3 c. honey
1/3 c. natural crunchy peanut butter
1 c. dry milk powder
1 c. carob chips
1 c. raw pecans, chopped
1 t. water

Put honey into a small saucepan and bring to a boil over high heat. Cook 30 seconds, then add remaining ingredients and stir well.

Scrape mixture onto cutting board or counter coated with about 1/4 c. dry milk powder. Shape into a ball, then roll into a 1" thick log and let cool for 10 minutes. Slice into 1/4" thick pieces. The outside of the log is coated with milk powder and when cut, the white surface "cracks" and looks like a real "uptown" treat!

COCOA NUT FUDGE

1 c. natural peanut butter
1 c. honey
1 c. dry milk powder
1 t. vanilla extract
1 c. carob or Wonderslim® cocoa powder
2 c. raw walnuts or pecans, chopped

Mix all ingredients together and press onto a plate, or form into balls and roll in extra nuts or coconut.

SESAME HONEY CANDY

1 c. honey
1 t. white vinegar
1 t. vanilla extract
1 c. sesame seeds, plain or toasted

Boil honey and vinegar to hard crack stage, about 300° F, being careful not to let mixture burn. Remove from heat, add vanilla and sesame seeds. Pour into lightly oiled pan. When slightly cooled but still warm, cut into small squares.

PISTACHIO HONEY SQUARES

1 c. honey
1 t. white vinegar
1 t. vanilla extract
1 c. pistachios, chopped

Boil honey and vinegar to hard crack stage, about 300° F, being careful not to let mixture burn. Remove from heat, add vanilla and pistachios. Place in lightly oiled pan and cut into squares when slightly cooled but still warm.

CLAIR'S FAVORITE PECAN BRITTLE

2 c. Demarara sugar* or Sucanat
1 c. light honey
1 c. water
1/2 t. salt
2 c. raw pecans
2 T. butter
2 t. baking soda

Combine sugar, honey, water and salt in a heavy saucepan until sugar dissolves. Cook over medium heat to soft ball stage (234°). Cook to hard crack stage (290°), adding pecans at 250° and stir often. Remove from heat. Quickly stir in butter and soda. Beat to a froth for a few seconds. Pour at once onto 2 well-buttered baking sheets, spreading with spatula. If desired, cool slightly and pull with forks to stretch thin. Makes about 1 1/2 pounds. *See p. 18.

MARSHMALLOW SQUARES

1 c. Sucanat
3/4 c. honey
1 1/2 T. unflavored gelatin
1/3 c. water
1/4 t. sea salt
1 t. vanilla extract

Pour water into a small saucepan. Sprinkle gelatin on top and let sit for 5 minutes. Place pan over medium heat and add remaining ingredients, except vanilla. Cook while stirring constantly to keep from boiling, until temperature reaches about 220°F, using a candy thermometer, or for about 10-12 minutes.

Add vanilla and transfer hot mixture to a bowl and beat with an electric mixer until cool, very thick and tacky*. Beat several minutes to produce a thick, marshmallow cream consistency.

Add 2 c. nuts and/or dried fruit if desired. Pour into pan and spread evenly. Let stand a few hours to set before cutting with a hot or buttered knife. Or, place in the freezer for 20 minutes.

For a more firm, nougat-like consistency, cook the mixture for 14-15 minutes, or until the temperature reaches about 225°F.

*For a quick beating option, place bowl containing hot marshmallow mixture in a larger bowl containing ice and cold water. Beat with electric mixer, being careful not to get ice water into mixture.

Variations:
Roll squares in toasted unsweetened coconut, nuts, or dip in melted carob. For an extra tasty treat, do a little of all three!
1) Stir in 1 c. carob or chocolate chips before spreading on a lightly oiled plate.
2) Stir in 3/4 –1 c. toasted almond slivers before spreading on a lightly oiled plate, and/or roll in toasted almond slivers after cooling time.
3) Stir in 3-3 1/2 c. granola before spreading on a lightly oiled plate. Cover hands with butter or oil and pat down evenly in baking dish.

PEANUT MARSHMALLOW SQUARES

1 recipe Marshmallow Squares
1/2 c. natural peanut butter
1/4 c. roasted, unsalted peanuts, chopped

Mix peanut butter and peanuts into marshmallow recipe just before transferring to mixing bowl.

Variation:

Use almond butter and chopped almonds for a different flavor.

Stir in 3-3 1/2 c. Uncle Sam® Toasted Whole Wheat Flakes and Flaxseed Cereal or other whole grain cereal to a half recipe of Peanut Marshmallow Squares before spreading in a lightly oiled baking dish. Coat hands with olive oil and press evenly into baking dish.

PEANUT BUTTER TOFFEE

1 c. honey
1/4 c. dry milk powder
2/3 c. natural peanut butter
2 t. vanilla extract
1 c. carob or chocolate chips
1 1/2 c. raw walnuts, chopped

Boil honey in a saucepan over high heat to hard ball stage (about 260° F). To test hard ball stage without a thermometer: Drop a few drops of mixture into a small glass of cold water. The drops should stay together and form a firm ball, or set up immediately. Once hard ball stage is reached, remove from heat and stir in dry milk. Then add peanut butter and vanilla; stir until combined. Pour immediately onto lightly oiled baking sheet*. Spread very thin, about 1/4". Sprinkle chips evenly over top and spread around as they melt. Press nuts into the carob/chocolate layer. Score and chill, then break into pieces. Keep refrigerated.

Variation: **Almond Butter Toffee** – substitute almond butter and chopped almonds for peanut butter and walnuts.

*If using a full baking sheet, double the recipe so the candy does not get too thin.

COOKIES, BARS, AND MUFFINS

Everyone loves the wonderful aroma of freshly baked cookies and muffins! Most of these wholesome recipes can be made ahead and frozen.

Our favorites in this section were originally called sugarplums. Remember the Christmas poem where "visions of sugarplums danced in their wee little heads"? These sweet treats are made with dried fruits and nuts...very nutritious, so delicious, and SO easy to make. They're packed with energy too!

NO-BAKE COOKIES

HONEY KRISPIES

1/2 c. honey
1/2 c. natural peanut butter
1/2 t. vanilla extract
1 c. dry milk powder
1 c. Uncle Sam® Toasted Whole-Wheat Flakes and Flaxseed Cereal*

Bring honey to a boil, and cook for 1 minute. Stir in peanut butter, vanilla, dry milk, and cereal. Remove from heat and let cool for a few minutes. Place on a surface dusted with milk powder and roll into a ball. Divide into fourths and roll into logs 12-14" long and about 1" in diameter. Cut into bite-sized pieces.

*If you can't find Uncle Sam® cereal, any crunchy whole grain cereal will work for this recipe.

NO-BAKE CHOCOLATE COOKIES

1/2 c. Sucanat
2 T. Wonderslim® cocoa or carob powder
2 T. soymilk
1 1/2 T. butter
1/4 c. natural creamy peanut butter
1/2 c. rolled oats
1 t. vanilla extract

Combine Sucanat, cocoa, soymilk and butter in medium saucepan. Bring to a full rolling boil over medium heat, stirring constantly. Stir in remaining ingredients. Drop 1 T. hot mixture at a time onto baking sheet lined with waxed paper. Chill until firm and refrigerate leftovers. Makes about 1 dozen cookies.
Variation: Stir in 1/3 c. raisins before cooking.

HONEY NO-BAKE COOKIES

These are a very "believable" version of the traditional no-bakes that are high in fat and loaded with sugar. We love them!

1/2 c. honey
1/4 c. butter
3 T. Wonderslim® cocoa or carob powder
2/3 c. natural peanut butter
2 c. quick oats
2 t. vanilla extract

Boil honey and butter for 1 minute. Stir in cocoa powder, peanut butter, oats, and vanilla. Spoon mixture onto waxed paper and divide into 24 mounds. Place in freezer for about an hour.

Variations:

Coconut No-Bakes - Reduce oats to 1 1/2 c. and add 1/2 c. unsweetened coconut.

Raisin No-Bakes - Boil 1/2 c. raisins with butter and honey.

Date and Nut No-Bakes - Add 1 c. chopped raw pecans along with the oats. During the last 30 seconds of cooking, add 2/3 c. chopped dates to honey and butter mixture and mix well.

Jam Thumbprint Cookies - Press thumb into the center of each cookie, and place about 1 teaspoon all-fruit strawberry jam in each indentation.

BERRY GOOD NO-BAKES

1/2 c. honey
1/4 c. butter
1/2 c. natural peanut butter
2 T. Nutri Fruit™ freeze-dried black raspberry powder*
2 1/4 c. quick oats
2 t. vanilla extract

Boil honey and butter for 1 minute. Stir in peanut butter, berry powder, oats, and vanilla. Spoon onto wax paper and divide into 24 mounds. Put in freezer for about an hour.
*See page 18 for ordering information.

PB&J NO-BAKES

1/2 c. honey
1/4 c. butter
1/4 c. natural peanut butter
2/3 c. 100% fruit juice sweetened strawberry jam
2 1/4 c. quick oats
2 t. vanilla extract

Boil honey and butter for 1 minute. Stir in peanut butter, strawberry jam, oats, and vanilla. Spoon onto wax paper and divide into 24 mounds. Put in freezer for about an hour.

SAUCEPAN COOKIES

1/2 c. Sucanat
3 T. butter
1 egg
1/4 c. raisins
1/4 c. pitted prunes
1/2 c. chopped raw nuts
1 t. vanilla extract
3/4 c. Uncle Sam® Toasted Whole-Wheat Flakes and Flaxseed Cereal*
1 c. unsweetened coconut

Put Sucanat, butter, and egg into a small saucepan and beat well with a spoon. In food processor, combine raisins and prunes and process until smooth, then spoon into saucepan and cook over high heat for 2 minutes, stirring constantly. Mixture will bubble, then turn darker and get thicker. When fruit blends in well, remove from heat and add nuts, vanilla, and cereal and stir well. Place 1/2 c. of coconut on cutting board. Spoon mixture onto coconut and pour remaining coconut on top. Press into a 1/2" thick square and cut, or roll into balls.

*Or any whole grain "flake" cereal.

BAKED COOKIES

HEALTH NUT COOKIES

1 1/3 c. whole wheat flour
1/4 t. cinnamon
1/2 t. sea salt
3/4 c. raisins
1/2 c. raw sunflower seeds
1 c. rolled oats
1/2 t. each baking soda and baking powder
1/2 c. raw walnuts, chopped
2 T. grated orange rind
2 T. orange juice concentrate
3/4 c. honey
1 egg
2 t. vanilla extract

Combine dry ingredients and then add remaining ingredients. Bake on a lightly oiled baking sheet at 350° F for 12 minutes, or until light brown. Makes about 40 medium-size cookies.

ONE AND ONE-HALF COOKIES
These cookies got their name because they contain 1 egg and 1/2 of everything else!

1 egg
1/2 c. Sucanat
1/2 c. natural crunchy peanut butter
1/2 t. vanilla extract
1/2 c. quick oats
1/2 c. carob or chocolate chips

Place all ingredients in a small mixing bowl and stir until well combined. Shape into 1" balls and place on a lightly oiled baking sheet. Flatten with a fork dipped in Sucanat. Bake at 350° for 9-10 minutes. Makes 24 cookies.

Variation: **One and One-Half Raisin-Nut Cookies** - To original recipe, add 1/2 c. raisins or dates and 1/2 c. chopped pecans and stir until well combined.

Peanut Butter Cookies

1/3 c. applesauce
2 T. canola oil
1 egg
2/3 c. peanut butter
1/2 t. vanilla extract
1 t. baking powder
1/2 t. baking soda
1/4 t. sea salt
1 c. Sucanat
1 1/4 c. whole wheat flour

Add ingredients in order listed and mix well. Drop by tablespoonful onto a baking sheet and press flat with tines of a fork or with your fingers. Bake at 350° F for 10-12 minutes. Makes 2 dozen cookies.
Variation: **Snowy Peanut Butter Cookies** – roll cookie dough in powdered evaporated cane juice before baking.

Excellent Oatmeal Chocolate Chip Cookies

1/3 c. Sucanat
1/3 c. honey
1 T. butter
1/4 c. unsweetened applesauce
1 egg
1/2 t. hot water
1 t. vanilla extract
1/2 t. baking soda
1/2 t. sea salt
3/4 c. whole wheat flour
1 c. quick oats
1/4 c. chopped raw pecans or walnuts
1/3 c. carob or chocolate chips

Combine butter and Sucanat, and then add remaining wet ingredients. Gradually mix in dry ingredients. Drop by spoonfuls onto an oiled baking sheet. Bake at 350° F for 14-16 minutes. Makes 2 dozen medium-size cookies.
Variation: For softer, more rounded cookies, add 1/4 c. olive oil with liquids. Bake for 13-14 minutes.

PUMPKIN COOKIES

3/4 c. Sucanat
1/2 c. honey
1/4 c. butter
1/4 c. unsweetened applesauce or oil
2 eggs
1 c. cooked or canned pumpkin
2 c. whole wheat flour
2 t. vanilla extract
1/4 t. sea salt
1/2 t. each nutmeg, ginger, cloves
1 1/2 t. cinnamon
2 t. baking powder
1 c. chopped raw walnuts

Combine ingredients in order listed. Mix well, and drop by spoonfuls onto an oiled baking sheet. Flatten slightly with spoon. Bake at 350° F for 15 minutes. Makes about 2 dozen cookies.
Variation: **Pumpkin Chocolate Chip Cookies** – stir in 2/3 c. chocolate or carob chips.

GINNI'S GINGERSNAPS

2 T. butter
1/2 c. Sucanat
1 egg
1/2 c. honey
2 T. blackstrap molasses
1 1/2 t. vinegar
2 c. whole wheat flour
1/2 t. baking soda
1/2 t. sea salt
1/4 t. cinnamon
2 T. powdered ginger
Pinch cayenne

Preheat oven to 350° F. Combine wet ingredients in a mixing bowl and then add dry ingredients, stirring well. Drop by spoonfuls onto a lightly oiled baking sheet. For chewy cookies, bake for 9-10 minutes; for snappy cookies, bake for 13-15 minutes. Makes about 4 dozen cookies.

JUMBLE COOKIES

1 c. natural chunky peanut butter
1/4 c. unsweetened applesauce or olive oil
1/2 c. honey
1 egg
1 1/2 c. whole wheat flour
1/2 c. regular or quick oatmeal
1 t. baking powder
1/2 c. peanuts
3/4 c. carob or chocolate chips

Preheat oven to 350° F. Cream the peanut butter, oil/applesauce, and honey. Mix in egg, then the dry ingredients. Drop by spoonfuls onto a lightly oiled baking sheet and bake for 8-12 minutes. Makes 2 dozen.

CHOCOLATE RAISIN BALLS

These are delightful wheat- and dairy-free cookies!

1/2 c. garbanzo bean flour
1/4 c. potato flour*
2 T. white bean flour
1/2 c. carob or Wonderslim® cocoa powder
1 t. baking powder
1 t. baking soda
1/4 t. sea salt
1/4 c. olive oil
1/4 c. unsweetened applesauce or mashed banana
3/4 c. Sucanat
1 t. vanilla extract
1 1/2 t. EnerG® Egg Replacer*
2 T. water
1/2 c. raisins
1/2 c. carob or chocolate chips
1 T. vinegar

Add in order given except for vinegar and mix well. Add vinegar and mix again. Drop by tablespoonful onto lightly oiled baking sheet. Bake at 350° F for 15-16 minutes. Makes 2 dozen.

Variation: **Chocolate Peanut Butter Balls** – Add 1/4 c. peanut butter to mixture and stir well.

*Available at health food stores.

Old Fashioned Oatmeal Cookies

1/2 c. Sucanat
1/3 c. honey
2 T. butter
1/3 c. unsweetened applesauce
1 egg
2 t. vanilla extract
1/2 t. baking powder
1/2 t. baking soda
1/2 t. cinnamon
1/4 t. nutmeg
1/8 t. powdered ginger
1/4 t. sea salt
1 c. whole wheat flour
1 c. quick oats

Combine Sucanat, honey and butter, then add applesauce, egg and vanilla. Gradually mix in dry ingredients. Drop by spoonfuls onto a lightly oiled baking sheet and bake at 375° F for 10-12 minutes. Makes 2 dozen medium cookies.
Variation: Add 1/2 c. raisins or other dried fruit.

Coconut Macaroons

2 eggs
1 1/3 c. unsweetened coconut - macaroon or ribbon
2 T. honey, or to taste
1/8 –1/4 t. almond extract

Preheat oven to 350° F. In a medium sized bowl, beat eggs until stiff. Add honey and almond extract and beat until stiff. Add coconut and mix well. Drop by tablespoonful onto an ungreased baking sheet and cook for 15-20 minutes, or until golden brown.

Life on the Go Bars (Sugarplums)

Sugarplums are a traditional English dessert that was popular before chocolate and refined sugar entered the scene. They can be made from just *raw nuts* (walnuts, almonds, pistachios, filberts, pecans) and *dried fruit* (raisins, dates, plums, apricots, apples, peaches, pears), or you can choose to add extras like flax, Juice Plus+ Complete® or other protein powder, vanilla or other flavorful extracts, honey, toasted nuts, coconut, cocoa or carob powder, or for special occasions, your favorite chocolate or carob chips, or mint chocolate chips.

My mother remembers her English grandmother making these, but she often hid a bit of medicine in the center for those in the family with constipation problems! Hmmm..are these the "spoonful of sugar that makes the medicine go down"?

As a child, these were the only treats I remember having. We called them "Nut and Raisin Balls." About once a week, my Dad would fasten a hand-operated meat grinder to our breakfast bar, and my sisters and I would take turns adding a handful of freshly shelled walnuts (organically grown, before we even knew how important that was!) and then a handful of raisins to the hopper of the grinder and turning the handle to crank out curly pieces of the mixture into a large pan.

When we had a sufficiently high mound, we then squeezed the mixture into 1" balls, eating our fill as we worked. Over the years, I've made these with a wide variety of different nuts, dried fruits and other add-ins. They're always a hit with everyone who tries them.

What a wonderfully *sneaky* way to supply good fats and fiber, plus the awesome nutrition of raw nuts and seeds!!

Our goal is to help you increase concentrated whole food nutrition, so we usually always add extra protein and nutrients in the form of Juice Plus+ Complete®, to turn these TREATS into a PORTABLE MEAL for our "Life on the Go" days (and for traveling). For more information on Complete®, see the Glossary, p. 19.

If you choose to use your own favorite brand of vanilla and chocolate protein powders, you'll need to adjust the amount called for in each recipe.

INSTRUCTIONS FOR ALL LIFE ON THE GO BARS:

In my food processor (I like the small but powerful Oskar 14081 - not the Oskar Jr.), I process all the ingredients for about 2 minutes, or until the mixture is no longer loose and chunky, but clumps together into a fairly smooth ball. You're basically making fruit and nut butter, which will be very similar in texture to peanut butter, but thick like a stiff cookie dough. If you have a large food processor, you may need to double these recipes.

The texture will vary, depending on the type of nut you choose, and how moist your dried fruit is. If the mixture is too dry after processing, add 1/2-1 t. water and pulse to mix in.

No matter what type of nut you use, some of the nut oil tends to "leak out" of these bars. You can remove it by blotting with a paper towel.

I usually make a batch, place it in a sandwich-size zip-top bag, flatten the mixture to about 1/2" thick, and then store flat in the refrigerator. Other options include pressing mixture onto a serving plate, and cutting it into squares or rolling the mixture into balls.* For a special treat, top with or roll in chopped, toasted nuts, coconut, Sucanat or dried cane juice, or powdered sugar. **Be creative! Experiment with whatever raw nuts, seeds, and dried fruits you have available.**

*Small balls look like "goat droppings" so I tease my grandchildren about bringing them "goaties" when I come to visit. Now I'm known as "Grandma Goatie"!

WALNUT RAISIN SUGARPLUMS (BASIC RECIPE)

1/2 c. raw walnuts
1/2 c. raisins, packed

Place all ingredients in food processor bowl and process for about 2 minutes, until mixture clumps together. Makes 2/3 c. For a chunkier Sugarplum, save half the nuts; add just before the end of processing.

Variations:
Vanilla Walnut Raisin Sugarplums: Add 2 T. Juice Plus+ Vanilla Complete® before processing.

Chocolate Walnut Raisin Sugarplums: Add 2 T. Juice Plus+ Chocolate Complete® before processing.
Full-O-Flax Walnut Raisin Sugarplums: Add 2 T. finely ground flax

seeds before processing for a treat that's higher in fiber, and loaded with Omega 3 fatty acids for better brain function, smoother skin, and a boatload of other benefits.

ALMOND DATE SUGARPLUMS

1/2 c. raw almonds
1/2 c. dates, packed (about 12)

Place almonds and dates in the food processor bowl and process about 2 minutes. (Almonds are harder than walnuts, and stay a little "chunky", rather than becoming smooth like walnuts.) Makes 2/3 c.

Variations:
Almond Raisin Sugarplums: Substitute raisins for dates.

Walnut Date Sugarplums: Substitute walnuts for almonds.

TRIPLE TREAT SUGARPLUMS

1/4 c. dates
1/4 c. dried plums (prunes)
1/4 c. raisins
3/4 c. walnuts

Place all ingredients in the food processor bowl and process about 2 minutes, or until the mixture is smooth. Makes about 1 c.

PEANUT BUTTER CHOCOLATE BITES

1/3 c. raw cashews
1/3 c. raisins
1 T. carob or Wonderslim® cocoa powder
1/2 t. vanilla extract
2 T. natural peanut butter

Place all ingredients in food processor bowl and process until mixture forms a smooth ball. Roll into small balls or press flat and cut into bite-sized pieces. Makes about 1/2 c.

CHOCOLATE RAISIN CASHEW BITES

3/4 c. raisins
1 c. raw cashews
1/4 c. (1 scoop) Juice Plus+ Chocolate Complete®
1 t. vanilla extract
1 T. carob or Wonderslim® cocoa powder

Place all ingredients in food processor bowl and process until mixture forms a ball. Roll into small balls or press flat and cut into bite-sized pieces. Makes about 1 1/3 c.

OMEGA 3 BARS

Walnuts and flax seeds are both very high in essential Omega 3 fatty acids

3/4 c. raisins
1/2 c. raw walnuts
1/4 c. (1 scoop) Juice Plus+ Vanilla Complete®
2 T. ground flax seeds
1/2 t. vanilla extract

Place all ingredients in food processor bowl and process for about 2 minutes, until mixture forms a ball. Press 1/2" thick, top with toasted walnuts, and cut into bite-sized pieces. Makes about 3/4 c.

APRICOT BARS

If you like apricots, you'll LOVE the taste of these. Because we cooked the honey, these bars have the texture of a _real_ candy bar!

1 lb. dried apricots
1/2 c. raw hazelnuts (filberts)
1/2 c. raw cashews
1/2 c. (2 scoops) Juice Plus+ Vanilla Complete®
1/2 t. vanilla extract
1/4 c. honey

Place all but honey in food processor bowl. Cook honey for 1 minute in a saucepan on medium-high heat, then pour into food processor bowl containing remaining ingredients. Process for about 2 minutes, until mixture forms a ball. Roll into balls or press flat and cut into bite-sized pieces. Makes about 2 c.

BROWNIE BITES

3/4 c. raw pecans or walnuts
3/4 c. raisins
1/4 c. (1 scoop) Juice Plus+ Chocolate Complete®
3 T. natural peanut butter
1 T. carob or Wonderslim® cocoa powder (or 1 1/2 t. of each)
1 t. vanilla extract

Place all ingredients in food processor bowl and process for about 2 minutes, until mixture forms a ball. Roll into balls or press into 1/2" thick bars and cut into bite-sized pieces. Makes about 3/4 c.

BLONDIE BITES

3/4 c. golden raisins
1/2 c. raw walnuts
1/4 c. (1 scoop) Juice Plus+ Vanilla Complete®
1/2 t. vanilla extract

Place all ingredients in food processor bowl and process for about 2 minutes, until mixture forms a ball. Press 1/2" thick and cut into bite-sized pieces. Makes about 3/4 c.

NUTTY RASPBERRY BROWNIE BITES

1/4 c. (1 scoop) Juice Plus+ Chocolate Complete®
1 t. vanilla extract
1/2 c. raw cashews
1 T. Nutri Fruit™ freeze-dried black raspberry powder
1/2 c. raisins, packed

Place all ingredients in food processor bowl and process for about 2 minutes, until mixture forms a ball. Roll into balls or press 1/2" thick and cut into bite-sized pieces. Makes about 2/3 c.

Variations: **Peanut Butter Raspberry Bites** – add 2 T. natural peanut butter. You can also substitute Juice Plus+ Vanilla Complete® in place of Chocolate Complete® for **Blondie Raspberry Bites**.

CHOCO-MALTED BROWNIE BARS

1/3 c. ground flax seeds
1/2 c. (2 scoops) Juice Plus+ Chocolate Complete®
1/3 c. raw walnuts
1/3 c. malted milk powder
1/8 t. Stevia powder (opt.)
2/3 c. raisins
1/3 c. dates
2 t. vanilla extract

Place all ingredients in food processor bowl and process for 2 minutes, or until ingredients form a ball. Press 1/2" thick onto a plate and cut into squares. Makes about 1 1/3 c.

COLE'S DOUBLE NUT DATE BARS

1/2 c. pitted dates, packed
1/2 c. raw cashews
1/4 c. (1 scoop) Juice Plus+ Chocolate Complete®
1 t. carob or Wonderslim® cocoa powder
1/2 t. vanilla extract
1/4 c. natural chunky peanut butter

Place all ingredients except peanut butter in food processor bowl and process for about 2 minutes. Add peanut butter and pulse to mix in. Place on plate and press 1/2" thick. These are also excellent topped with toasted, salted, finely chopped cashews or peanuts. Makes 1 c.

CHOCOLATE CASHEW DATE BARS

1/2 c. raw cashews
1/2 c. dates, chopped
1/4 c. (1 scoop) Juice Plus+ Chocolate Complete®
1 t. carob or Wonderslim® cocoa powder
1/2 t. vanilla extract
1/4 c. toasted, salted almonds (opt.)

Place all ingredients except almonds in food processor bowl and process for about 2 minutes, or until ingredients form a ball. Press onto a plate and top with almonds, if used. Cut into squares. Makes 3/4 c.

CASHEW, DATE AND RAISIN BARS

An excellent source of Omega 3 fatty acids.

1/3 c. raw cashews
1/2 c. dates
1/2 c. raisins
1/4 c. almond butter
1/4 c. (1 scoop) Juice Plus+ Chocolate Complete®
1/3 c. ground flax seeds
1/2 t. vanilla extract

Combine ingredients in food processor bowl and process about 2 minutes, until mixture forms a ball. Press onto a plate and cut into squares. Makes about 1 1/4 c.

DAILY ENERGY BARS

Because these bars are high in protein as well as both soluble and insoluble fiber, they are guaranteed to provide a nutritious, long-lasting source of energy. For an extra special treat, you can drizzle the cut bars with melted carob or chocolate chips.

2 T. ground flax seed
1/3 c. mixed prunes and raisins
2 T. Juice Plus+ Vanilla Complete®
1/2 c. raw walnuts
6 Juice Plus+ Chocolate Fudge Thins®
2 t. vanilla extract
1 t. carob or Wonderslim® cocoa powder

Place all ingredients in food processor bowl and process for about 2 minutes, or until ingredients form a ball. Press onto a plate and cut into bars. Makes about 2/3 c.

*Juice Plus+ Thins® are an excellent source of fiber and nutrients. See p. 19 for more information.

PLUM DELICIOUS PEANUT BUTTER BITES

The plums (alias prunes!) add a surprisingly delicious flavor to the recipe.

1/2 c. dried plums (prunes)
1/2 c. (2 scoops) Juice Plus+ Chocolate Complete®
1/2 c. raw walnuts or cashews
1/2 c. raisins
1/4 c. natural peanut butter
1/4 c. ground flax seeds
1 t. vanilla extract
1 t. carob or Wonderslim® cocoa powder

Place all ingredients in food processor bowl and process for about 2 minutes, or until ingredients form a ball. Press onto a plate and cut into squares. Makes about 1 1/4 c.

KATON'S ALMOND BITES

1 c. raw almonds
1 c. raisins
1/4 c. (1 scoop) Juice Plus+ Vanilla Complete®
1 t. vanilla extract

Put all ingredients in food processor. Process until mixture is well combined and will hold together well. Flatten out and cut into pieces or roll into balls. Can also be rolled in more chopped almonds, if desired. Makes about 1 1/3 c.

Variation: **Almond Chocolate Chip Bars** - add 1 c. carob or chocolate chips to mixture and process as previously described. This mixture is also good as a cookie filling - sandwich a ball of mixture between two cookies of your choice. Tasty!

KELSEY'S PISTACHIO BITES

Using the Almond Bites recipe above, substitute pistachios for a wonderful, sweet and slightly salty treat.

CHOCO-DATE FIBER BARS

These bars supply good fats and fiber from raw nuts and raw flax.

10 raw almonds
2 T. flax seeds
4 Juice Plus+ Chocolate Fudge Thins®
1/4 c. mashed dates
Toasted nuts
Unsweetened coconut

Grind almonds, flax, and Thins® to a fine powder in blender or small electric coffee mill. Place in food processor bowl and add dates. (If they are hard to mash, cover with hot water, then pour it off and let them sit a few minutes.) Mix well to form a firm paste. Roll in nuts and coconut, then press into bars or roll into balls. These are great for a mid-morning and mid-afternoon snack! They also make great travel snacks. (May be sweetened with a *tiny* pinch of Stevia powder.) Makes about 1/2 c.

*Juice Plus+ Chocolate Fudge Thins® are tasty fiber-containing wafers. See p. 19 for more information.

APPLE-DATE FIBER BARS

10 raw almonds
2 T. flax seeds
4 Apple-Cinnamon Juice Plus+ Thins®
1/4 c. mashed dates
Toasted nuts
Unsweetened coconut

Grind almonds, flax, and Thins® to a fine powder in blender or small electric coffee mill. Place in food processor bowl and add dates. (If they are hard to mash, cover with hot water, then pour it off and let them sit a few minutes.) Mix well to form a firm paste. Roll in nuts and coconut, then press into bars or roll into balls. These are great for a mid-morning and mid-afternoon snack! They also make great travel snacks. Makes about 1/2 c.

*Juice Plus+ Apple-Cinnamon Thins® are tasty fiber-containing wafers. See p. 19 for more information.

LEMON BARS

Crust:
3/4 c. whole wheat flour
1/2 c. raw walnuts, finely ground
1 T. butter
1/4 c. unsweetened applesauce
1 T. Sucanat

Filling:
2 eggs
1/4 c. unsweetened applesauce
1/2 c. honey
1 T. lemon zest
5 T. fresh lemon juice

Mix crust ingredients together and press into a lightly oiled 8x8" square pan. Bake at 325° F for 20-25 minutes. Allow to cool. Meanwhile, combine filling ingredients and beat until smooth. Pour into cooled crust and bake at 325° F for 20 minutes. When cooled, cut into 2" squares. Dust with powdered Sucanat if desired. Makes about 16 squares.

BLENDER BROWNIES

1/4 c. olive oil
1/3 c. hot water
1/2 t. vanilla extract
1 egg
3/4 c. whole wheat flour
1/3 c. Wonderslim® cocoa powder
1/4 t. baking soda
1/2 c. Sucanat
1/8 t. sea salt
1/2 c. raw walnuts, chopped

Heat oven to 350° F. Add all ingredients except nuts to blender jar and pulse to blend just until smooth. Pour into lightly oiled 8x8" baking pan and sprinkle nuts on top. Bake for 30 minutes or until an inserted toothpick comes out clean. Cut into 2" squares.

Variation: Sprinkle 1/2 c. carob or chocolate chips over the top of baked brownies and spread after melted for a chocolatey frosting.

RASPBERRY OAT BARS

Crust and Topping:
1 3/4 c. rolled oats
1 1/4 c. whole wheat flour
1/4 c. white bean or
    garbanzo bean flour
1/2 t. baking soda
1/2 c. chopped nuts
1/2 t. sea salt
3/4 c. honey
3/4 c. applesauce

Sauce:
2 c. fresh or frozen raspberries
1/2 c. honey
3 T. water
2 T. cornstarch
2 t. lemon juice

Heat oven to 350° F. Combine dry ingredients. Add applesauce and honey, mixing until crumbly. Reserve 3/4 c. mixture; press remaining mixture onto bottom of 9x13" lightly oiled baking dish. Bake 8 minutes. Meanwhile, combine berries, honey, and 2 T. of the water in a saucepan. Bring to a boil; simmer for 2 minutes. Mix cornstarch, remaining water and lemon juice and gradually stir into berry mixture. Stir about 30 seconds or until thickened. Spread over baked mixture. Sprinkle reserved oat mixture over the top and bake for 15-18 minutes or until topping is golden brown. Let cool and cut into bars.

OAT AND BARLEY BARS

These tasty bars are wheat-free, but not gluten-free. It's best to avoid having wheat every day. Experiment with a variety of different grains. You'll be amazed at the variety of tastes and textures!

1 c. raisins
1 c. dates, chopped
1 c. raw hazelnuts or almonds, chopped
1 c. oat bran
1 c. oat flour
1/2 c. barley flour
1/2 c. barley malt powder (or malted milk powder)
1/2 c. honey, melted

Combine dry ingredients. Gradually pour in honey, mixing just until well blended. Press into a lightly oiled 9x13" pan. Bake 15-20 minutes at 350° F until golden brown. Cut into bars.

MUFFINS

MULTI-GRAIN MUFFINS

1 c. soymilk
3 T. honey
1/4 c. olive oil
1 egg
3/4 c. whole wheat flour
1/2 c. yellow cornmeal
1/2 c. quick oats
3 T. ground flax seeds
1 T. baking powder
1/2 t. sea salt
1/4 c. raw pecans, chopped

Preheat oven to 375° F. Combine wet ingredients in a large bowl and mix well. Gradually stir or beat in dry ingredients, adding pecans last. Spoon into 12-16 muffin cups and bake 24 minutes.

Variation: **Sweet Multi-Grain Muffins** – add 2 t. vanilla, 1/4 c. raisins, 1 t. cinnamon, and increase honey to 3/4 c.

PEANUT BUTTER BANANA MUFFINS

2 bananas
2/3 c. all natural chunky peanut butter
1/2 c. unsweetened applesauce
1/2 c. honey
1 egg
2 c. whole wheat flour
2 t. baking soda
1 t. baking powder
1/2 t. sea salt

Preheat oven to 350° F. Mash bananas with a fork or a potato masher until there are no large lumps. Add remaining wet ingredients, and then add dry ingredients. Mix well, and spoon into muffin cups. Bake for 20 minutes. Makes 12-16 muffins.

BANANA NUT MUFFINS

3 ripe bananas
1 egg
1/2 c. unsweetened applesauce*
1/2 c. honey
2 1/2 c. whole wheat flour
2 t. baking soda
1/2 t. baking powder
1/2 t. sea salt
1/2 t. nutmeg
1/2 c. each raw pecans and walnuts, chopped

Preheat oven to 350° F. Mash bananas with a fork or a potato masher until smooth. Add remaining wet ingredients, and then gradually add dry ingredients. Mix well, spoon into muffin tins lined with paper muffin cups and bake for 20 minutes. Makes approximately 24 muffins.

*If you don't use applesauce regularly, you can buy a large jar and freeze 1/4 c. portions in a muffin tin. When solid, place in a quart zip-top freezer bag. Thaw before adding to recipe ingredients.

CINNAMON CRUNCH MUFFINS

3 c. whole wheat flour
1 1/2 c. Sucanat
1/2 t. sea salt
2 t. cinnamon
1 t. ginger
1 t. nutmeg
1/2 c. olive oil
1 c. pecans, chopped

2 t. baking powder
1/2 t. baking soda
2 eggs
1/2 c. soymilk

Preheat oven to 375° F. Mix first 8 ingredients together and set 2/3 c. aside for topping, then add remaining ingredients and stir well. Spoon into muffin cups, and put approximately 1 T. of the topping on each muffin. Bake 25 minutes. Makes about 20 muffins.

CRISPY CRUNCHIES

We all love crunchy snacks and treats. We think you'll love these sweet or savory crackers and breads, as well as the seasoned nuts and seeds. They're delicious as well as nutritious.

They're great for snacking at school, at home, at the office, in the car, or on the trail. Don't leave home without yours!

Savory Crunchables

Alphabet Vegetables

Kids of all ages love raw vegetables when served with tasty dips. See the dip section for some great serving ideas.

Asparagus – spears
Bell peppers (green, red, yellow and orange) – sliced
Broccoli – florets
Carrots – sticks
Cauliflower – florets
Celery – sticks
Cherry tomatoes – leave whole
Cucumber – sticks and rounds
Green beans – remove ends
Jicama – slices and sticks
Mushrooms – leave small ones whole, cut large ones in half
Napa cabbage – leaves
Radishes – whole or slice into each side to make "petals"
Sugar snap peas/Snow peas – whole or slivers
Sweet Potatoes/Yams – sticks and rounds
Yellow squash – sticks and rounds
Zucchini – sticks and rounds

Crispy Potato Wedges

4 medium potatoes, cut in 1/2-3/4" thick wedges
Season-All® Seasoned salt* to taste

Place potato wedges in mixing bowl and sprinkle with Season-All®. Place wedges skin-side down on baking sheet, either lightly coated with olive oil, covered with parchment paper, or on a silicone baking mat**. Bake in a preheated oven at 450° F for 20-25 minutes, until wedges blister and are golden brown.

*Season-All® does not contain MSG, artificial flavorings or colorings.

**The Matfer® Exopat Nonstick Baking Sheet is a silicone mat that is placed on a baking sheet and eliminates need for parchment paper or nonstick cooking surfaces. It wipes clean with a sponge and can be found at www.villagekitchen.com or www.amazon.com. These sheets costs only about $12 each, and are well worth the investment!

BASIC CRACKERS

1/2 c. water
3/4 t. sea salt
2 t. Season-All® Seasoned Salt*
3/4 c. corn flour
1 1/3 c. whole wheat flour
1/4 c. butter
1 t. baking powder

Mix just until ingredients are blended (the more you knead the dough, the tougher the crackers will be). Add only enough water to make a fairly stiff dough. Roll out on a floured surface with a lightly floured rolling pin. Cut into 2" squares and bake at 350° F for about 25 minutes, or until slightly brown and crisp.

Variations:
Garlic Italian Crackers - Omit seasoned salt and add 1 t. each Italian Seasoning, dried basil leaves, and garlic powder. Cook about 20 minutes; then sprinkle fresh or dried parmesan cheese over crackers. Cook 2 more minutes, or until cheese is melted.

Salsa Crackers - Omit seasoned salt, reduce water to 1/4 c. and add 1/4 c. salsa. Cook about 20 minutes. Or, for cheesy salsa crackers, sprinkle baked crackers with grated mozzarella cheese. Cook for 5 more minutes, or until cheese is melted.

Barbecue Crackers - Omit seasoned salt, reduce water to 1/3 c.; add 5 T. barbecue sauce and 1/8 t. paprika.

*Season-All® does not contain MSG, artificial flavorings or colorings. It's great on all vegetables, savory breads and crackers, popcorn, and even pasta.

CHILI CRACKERS

1/4 c. salsa
3/4 t. sea salt
3/4 c. corn flour
1 1/3 c. whole wheat flour
1/4 c. butter
1 t. baking powder
1/2 t. chili powder
1/2 t. onion powder
1/4 t. garlic powder
1/8 t. cumin
1/16 t. cayenne pepper
1/4 c. water

Mix just until ingredients are blended (too much kneading produces a tough cracker). Add only enough water to make a fairly stiff dough. Roll out on a floured surface with a lightly floured rolling pin. Bake at 350° F for about 20-25 minutes, or until slightly browned and crisp. Remove from oven and spray or brush tops lightly with olive oil and sprinkle with coarse sea salt. Cut or break into bite-sized pieces.

POPPED WHEAT AND SEEDS

1 c. raw wheat kernels
1/2 c. sunflower seeds
1/2 c. pumpkin seeds
1-3 t. chili powder
1-2 t. tamari soy sauce, or Bragg Liquid Aminos®

Pour dry wheat into a preheated heavy skillet (no oil) over medium high heat. When wheat begins to "pop", stir constantly. If wheat starts to get too brown, reduce heat to medium. When the seeds have all turned golden brown and popping has almost stopped, transfer to a bowl. Repeat with sunflower and pumpkin seeds. Sprinkle with 1-3 t. chili powder (depending on how spicy you like your mix), and enough tamari to make the chili powder stick to the seeds. Serve hot or cold. This mixture lasts for weeks without refrigeration.

We also like to add walnuts, pecans, and almonds (toasted in the skillet over medium heat, or in the oven). We usually toast a big batch of nuts and then freeze until ready to use.

ORIENTAL WHEAT AND SEED MIX

1 c. raw wheat kernels
1/2 c. sunflower seeds
1/2 c. pumpkin seeds
1/4-1/2 t. ginger
2 t. tamari, or Bragg Liquid Aminos®
1/2 t. olive oil
1/2 c. freeze-dried peas (opt.)
Sea salt to taste

Pour dry wheat into a preheated heavy skillet (no oil) over medium high heat. When wheat begins to "pop", stir constantly. If wheat starts to get too brown, reduce heat to medium. When the seeds have all turned golden brown and popping has almost stopped, transfer to a bowl. Repeat with sunflower and pumpkin seeds, and add to wheat. Stir in oil and seasonings, adding peas last, if used.

ROASTED NUTS AND SEEDS

This recipe can be made with one or many types of nuts and seeds. Our favorites are walnuts, cashews, pine nuts*, almonds, pecans, hazelnuts (filberts)*, pumpkin seeds*, and sunflower seeds*.

4 c. raw nuts or seeds
2 t. butter or olive oil
1 t. sea salt or Season-All® Seasoned Salt

Roast 3 cups of nuts or seeds on a baking sheet at 350° F for 20-25 minutes. Add remaining raw nuts and stir in butter or oil and salt or seasoning until evenly coated.
*These smaller seeds only need to cook for 10-12 minutes or until slightly browned.

ROASTED BLACK PEPPER CASHEWS

2 c. cashews
2 t. olive oil
1/2 t. black pepper
Scant 1/2 t. sea salt

Combine all ingredients in a bowl and stir to coat. (Cashews can be raw or roasted. To roast, place on a baking sheet and roast at 350° F for 20-25 minutes.)

GARLIC AND ONION CASHEWS

2 c. cashews
2 t. olive oil
1/2 t. garlic powder
1/2 t. onion powder
Sea salt to taste

Combine all ingredients in a bowl and stir to coat. (Cashews can be raw or roasted. To roast, place on a baking sheet and roast at 350° F for 20-25 minutes.) If desired, sprinkle nuts with cayenne pepper for an extra zing!

CHILI LIME CASHEWS

2 c. cashews
2 t. olive oil
2 t. chili powder
1/2 t. lime oil*
Sea salt to taste

Combine all ingredients in a bowl and stir to coat. (Cashews can be raw or roasted. To roast, place on a baking sheet and roast at 350° F for 20-25 minutes.) If desired, sprinkle nuts with cayenne pepper for an extra zing!

*Can be purchased at most health food stores.

GINGER MASALA CASHEWS

2 c. cashews
2 t. olive oil
1 t. powdered ginger
1/2 t. masala (a blend of Indian spices)*
1/2 t. garlic powder

Combine all ingredients in a bowl and stir to coat. (Cashews can be raw or roasted. To roast, place on a baking sheet and roast at 350° F for 20-25 minutes.) If desired, sprinkle nuts with cayenne pepper for an extra zing! Also, for a sweeter taste, add 1/2 c. white raisins to the cooled mixture.

*Can be found at most health food stores and some grocery stores.

TACO NUTS

2 c. cashews
2 t. olive oil
4 t. taco seasoning*

Combine all ingredients in a bowl and stir to coat. (Cashews can be raw or roasted. To roast, place on a baking sheet and roast at 350° F for 20-25 minutes.) If desired, sprinkle nuts with cayenne pepper for an extra zing!

*McCormick Taco Seasoning® does not contain MSG. If you'd rather make your own, the recipe follows.

TACO SEASONING MIX

4 t. dry onion flakes, minced or chopped
4 t. fine corn meal
2 t. sea salt
2 t. chili powder
2 t. paprika
1 t. ground cumin
1 t. cornstarch
1/2 t. oregano flakes
1/4 t. garlic powder
2 vegetable bouillon cubes, crushed

Mix together and store in labeled container.

SWEET CRUNCHABLES

SUCANUTS

1 c. raw cashews
2 T. Sucanat
1 t. olive oil
1/4 t. vanilla extract
Sprinkle of sea salt

Place cashews in a dry heavy skillet and toast over medium heat, stirring constantly until lightly browned. Stir in remaining ingredients and allow to cool. Makes 1 cup.

CINNAMON-SUCANAT WEDGES

2 pita breads or 4 flour tortillas
2 T. Sucanat
1/2 t. cinnamon

Preheat oven to 400° F. Combine Sucanat and cinnamon in a small bowl. Split pitas and place on a baking sheet. Spread pita with a small amount of butter or spray lightly with olive oil (no oil/butter needed on tortillas). Sprinkle with Sucanat and cinnamon mixture, then cut into pie-shaped wedges. Bake 5 minutes. Serve with Fruit Salsa (p. 88).

CRUNCHY ALMOND SNACKS

4 cups raw almonds
1 egg white
1/2 c. Sucanat
1 t. cinnamon
1 t. vanilla extract

Preheat oven to 225° F. In a large bowl, beat egg white until frothy. Add almonds and stir until evenly coated. Add remaining ingredients and stir well. Transfer to a lightly oiled baking sheet. Bake 40 minutes.

HONEYED CASHEWS

2 c. raw cashews
4 T. honey
4 t. sesame seeds
2 t. olive oil
2 t. vanilla extract

Place all ingredients except vanilla in small saucepan over medium-high heat. Stir well until mixture sizzles, then reduce to medium heat. Stir and cook until golden brown (about 2 minutes). Stir in vanilla and place on oiled plate to cool. If desired, sprinkle lightly with sea salt. Store in airtight container.

TRAIL MIX

1 c. raw cashews
1 c. raw walnuts
1 c. raw pecans
1 c. raw almonds
1 c. sunflower seeds
1 c. pumpkin seeds
1 c. raisins
1 c. golden raisins
1 c. carob or chocolate chips
2 t. sea salt
Vegetable oil spray*

Preheat oven to 350° F. Spread nuts on a baking sheet and spray lightly with vegetable oil. Sprinkle salt over nuts and stir well. Roast nuts 25 minutes, stirring once or twice to prevent burning. Remove from oven. When completely cool, transfer to a bowl and stir in raisins and chips.

Variation: If you have people in your family who invariably pick out the chips in the trail mix, then stir together the nuts, raisins, and chips while the nuts are still hot. The chips will melt and coat the whole mixture.

*Check at Wal-Mart or other discount stores for Oil-O-Pump™ by Gemco Ware Inc. It costs about $4 and works the same as the $15-20 brands. Fill it with your favorite healthful oil.

APPLE CINNAMON TRAIL MIX

1/2 c. pumpkin seeds
1/2 c. sunflower seeds
1/2 c. carob or chocolate chips
1/2 c. dehydrated apple pieces, cut into bite-sized chunks
1/2-1 t. cinnamon (or to taste)

Preheat oven to 350° F. Spread seeds on a baking sheet and roast nuts for 25 minutes, stirring once or twice to prevent burning around the edges. Remove from oven and while hot, transfer to a bowl or bag and stir in remaining ingredients. Mix well to coat all ingredients evenly as the chips melt.

APPLE CINNAMON CRACKERS

1/4 c. water
1/4 c. applesauce
1/4 c. butter
1 1/2 t. cinnamon
1/8 t. sea salt
1/8 t. nutmeg
1/3 c. Sucanat
3/4 c. corn flour*
1 1/3 c. whole wheat flour
1 t. baking powder

Add only enough water to make a fairly stiff dough. Mix just until ingredients are blended (the more you knead the dough, the tougher the crackers will be). Roll out on a floured surface with a rolling pin. Cut into 2" squares and sprinkle tops with a mixture of 1 T. Sucanat and 1 t. cinnamon. Bake at 350° F for 24-26 minutes, or until slightly brown and crisp.

*If you only have corn meal, grind it to a flour using a blender or small seed or coffee mill.

SUGAR CORN

1/4 c. popcorn kernels
1/2 c. Sucanat
1 T. butter
2 T. olive oil or organic canola oil
1 t. water

Pop popcorn and place in a medium to large bowl. In a saucepan, combine remaining ingredients and bring to a boil over high heat. Stir one minute (oil will separate, but that's normal). Pour over popped corn; then stir to break up chunks. Sprinkle with Butter Buds, or other butter-flavored seasoning to taste.

Variation: **Nutty Popcorn** - Add 1/4 c. chopped raw walnuts, 1/4 t. cinnamon, and 1 T. vanilla extract to saucepan after boiling. Pour over corn and stir to coat. Place on a baking sheet and bake 15 minutes at 350° F, stirring once about halfway through the cooking time. Remove from oven and let cool.

DIPS

Chips just can't resist these dips...especially the ones that are made with beans. What a tasty way to get your 1-2 servings of legumes every day!!!

Children love to dip veggies. Our favorites are carrots, celery, cucumbers, sweet potatoes, and peeled broccoli stems. Try a variety of different vegetables, and include lots of different colors.

Our sweet dips are a tasty way to encourage children and adults to eat more fresh fruit. Be sure to pick fruit that is ripe, which usually always means soft to the touch. Press lightly with your thumb, and if the fruit has a little "give" to it, it's ready to eat. It should also <u>smell</u> like fruit! If it was picked green, however, the flavor won't be as sweet as when allowed to ripen on the vine or the tree.

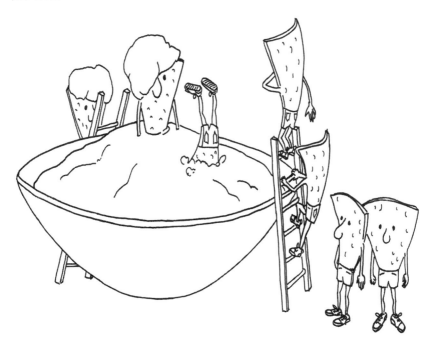

SAVORY DIPS

These dips are very versatile and taste great with veggies such as carrots, cucumbers, broccoli, cauliflower, radishes, celery, or Napa cabbage leaves. Crackers, rye crisps, chips, or breadsticks also taste great. Dips can be a tasty topping for a wrap or a pita sandwich too!

ORIGINAL HUMMUS DIP

2 c. cooked or canned garbanzo beans
2 T. fresh lemon juice
3 T. sesame tahini (or natural peanut butter)
3 1/2 T. water or reserved bean juice
1 large clove garlic
Sea salt and black pepper to taste

Put all in food processor and process until smooth. For an extra zing, add about 1/8 t. cayenne pepper.

EASY HUMMUS AND RED PEPPER DIP

1 c. cooked or canned garbanzo beans
1/2 c. cottage cheese (opt.)
1 large red bell pepper, quartered (with seeds removed)
1/2 garlic clove, minced
1/4 t. sea salt
1/8 t. black pepper

Combine all ingredients in food processor and process until smooth.

GREEN OLIVE HUMMUS DIP

1 15 oz. can garbanzo beans, drained
1/2 c. green olives
1/4 c. reserved bean juice
2 cloves garlic
Black pepper to taste

Combine all ingredients in food processor and blend until smooth.

BUTTERMILK RANCH DIP

1 1/2 c. Vegenaise® or mayonnaise
2 1/2 c. buttermilk
2 T. dried parsley
1 T. dried onion flakes
1/2-1 t. sea salt
1/2 t. garlic powder
1/2 t. black pepper

Place all ingredients in a mixing bowl or food processor. Stir or process just until smooth. Makes 1 quart. Serve with Alphabet Vegetables (p. 72). For a lower-fat version, reduce Vegenaise® to 1 c., and increase buttermilk to 3 c. Add 1/4-1/3 tsp. xanthan gum and blend to thicken.

Note: Fresh or dried chives may be substituted for parsley.

Variation: **Spicy Hot Dip** – add 1/4 c. mild or hot Picanté sauce.

THOUSAND ISLAND DIP

1 c. Vegenaise® or mayonnaise
1/4 c. catsup
1 T. finely chopped dill pickles
Dash Worcestershire sauce

Thoroughly mix Vegenaise® , then stir in remaining ingredients. Serve cold. Makes 1 1/4 cups. Serve with Alphabet Vegetables (p. 72) or Crispy Potato Wedges (p. 72).

CREAMY CHIVE DIP

1/2 c. cottage cheese
1/4 c. yellow or white onion
2 T. minced chives
1 small garlic clove
1/4 t. sea salt

Combine all ingredients in a food processor and process until smooth.

Tomato Basil Dip

1/4 c. cottage cheese
1 small clove garlic
1/2 c. canned or fresh tomato dices*
6 large basil leaves, chopped
1 t. lemon juice
1/2 t. sea salt (optional)
A sprinkle of black pepper

Blend cottage cheese and garlic in a food processor. Add remaining ingredients and pulse to mix, just until slightly chunky.

*If using canned tomatoes, I recommend Hunt's® Diced Tomatoes with Basil, Garlic, and Oregano.

Cucumber Yogurt Dip

1/3 c. plain yogurt
3 T. grated cucumber
1-2 large garlic cloves, minced
1/8 t. sea salt
1 t. lemon juice

Grate cucumber and pat dry with a paper towel. Add to remaining ingredients and serve with pita bread, cucumbers, or whatever else sounds good to you. This is a favorite sauce in India. We love it with even *more* fresh minced garlic for extra zing!

Cool Cucumber Dip

1/2 c. cucumber dices
1/2 c. plain yogurt
3/4 t. sea salt
1/4 t. xanthan gum
8 mint leaves

Combine all ingredients in a food processor and process until smooth.

Cucumber Guacamole

1 medium sized cucumber, grated
2 large tomatoes, diced
1 large avocado, mashed
2 garlic cloves, minced
2 T. lime or lemon juice
1/2 t. sea salt

Combine all ingredients, stirring gently.

Bingham's Fresh Salsa

4 large fresh tomatoes, cubed
1 large onion, chopped
1 small yellow bell pepper, diced
1 c. chopped cilantro, stems removed
1-2 cloves garlic, minced
Juice of 2 limes
1 1/2 t. sea salt
1 small jalapeno pepper* (Add more if you like yours hot!)

Combine all ingredients in a blender jar or food processor and pulse to blend until just slightly chunky.
*We like to make a large batch and use a variety of peppers for added flavor.

Quick 'N Easy Bean Dip

1 15 oz. can pinto or black beans
1/4 c. salsa
1/2 t. chili powder
2 T. water or bean juice
Salt and pepper to taste

Combine all ingredients in a food processor and process until fairly smooth. For a hot dip, just heat through and serve. Makes 1 cup. This dip is great as it is, but if you prefer, you can add grated cheese or sour cream (regular or soy).

RITA'S FAMOUS 5-MINUTE BEAN DIP

2 1/4 c. water
3/4 c. pinto or black bean flour*
1/2 - 3/4 t. sea salt
1/2 t. chili powder
1/4 t. cumin
1/16 t. garlic powder (opt.)
3/4 c. Pace® Picanté sauce

Bring water to a boil in a small saucepan. Whisk in dry ingredients. Cook, while stirring, over medium heat for 1 minute, or until mixture thickens. Reduce heat to low, cover pan, and cook 4 minutes. Stir in Picanté sauce. Mixture thickens as it cools and will stay thick even after reheating. Serve with low- or no-fat chips, or use as burrito filling.

*Purchase Bob's Red Mill bean flours, or grind dry beans to a flour using an electric grain mill such as the K-TEC Kitchen Mill® or the WonderMill® (the improved Whisper Mill).

SWEET DIPS

These sweet dips are often made with fruit and/or yogurt. They are great for dipping fruit such as strawberries, grapes, apples, or pineapple. They also go well with crackers or rice cakes.

Most of these dips include xanthan gum, which is a thickening agent. You can also use Clear-Jel®, Ultra Gel® or guar gum*. All of these products thicken liquids without the use of heat and can be found at most health food stores.

*If your favorite health food store doesn't have guar gum in their bulk food section, NOW® brand is usually the least expensive.

CITRUS FRUIT DIP

1/2 c. plain yogurt
2 t. lemon juice
1/4 t. lemon zest
1 T. orange juice concentrate
1 T. honey
3/4 t. xanthan gum

Combine all ingredients in food processor and process until smooth.

RED RASPBERRY FRUIT DIP

1/2 c. fresh or frozen raspberries
1/3 c. Welch's® 100% White Grape Raspberry Concentrate
1/4 t. xanthan gum

Combine all ingredients in the blender and blend until thickened, about 1 minute. Dip apple slices, or drizzle over sliced bananas, green grapes, or fresh peaches. Makes about 2/3 c.

STRAWBERRY DIP

5-6 large strawberries, sliced
1/2 c. plain yogurt
1-2 T. honey (depending on the sweetness of your strawberries)
1/2 t. vanilla extract
1/4 t. xanthan gum

Combine all ingredients in the processor and process until smooth.

PEANUT BUTTER YOGURT DIP
This is a really good dip for apple slices or crackers!

1/2 c. plain yogurt
1/2 c. natural creamy peanut butter
2-3 T. honey
1 t. cinnamon
1 t. vanilla extract

Combine all ingredients and mix well.

SWEET MINT DIP

2/3 c. plain yogurt
1/4 c. honey
8 mint leaves
2 t. lime juice
1/4 t. xanthan gum

Combine all ingredients in a food processor and process until smooth and mint leaves are reduced to small specks. Serve with strawberries, melons, grapes, or mangoes.

PIÑA COLADA DIP

1/2 c. plain yogurt
1/2 c. crushed pineapple
2 T. unsweetened coconut
2 t. honey
1/2 t. xanthan gum
1/4 t. vanilla extract

Combine all ingredients in food processor and process until smooth.

FRUIT SALSA

2 Golden Delicious apples
2 t. lime or lemon juice
3 kiwis, peeled and chopped
1 c. chopped strawberries
1 c. chopped peaches
2 T. honey*

Chop apples into very small pieces and place in a mixing bowl with lime or lemon juice. Add remaining fruit and honey and stir until well mixed. Serve with Cinnamon-Sucanat Wedges (p. 78) or Apple Cinnamon Crackers (p. 80).

*Adjust honey to taste depending on sweetness of fruit.

SNACK WRAPS

Wraps are great for breakfast, lunch, or dinner because they are so versatile. Best of all, they make a great snack! They can be filled with green salads, cooked grains, tofu, eggs, or meat. Choose your favorite salad dressing or salsa, or make your own to top it all off.

Make your own homemade wraps from this section, or buy one of the following at the grocery store:

> *Corn tortillas (warmed in toaster, toaster oven or skillet)*
> *Whole wheat flour tortillas*
> *Pita Pockets*
> *Flatbreads*

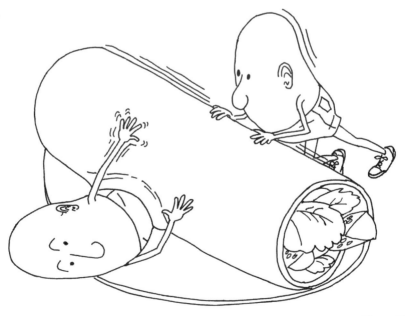

PITA POCKETS

3 1/2-4 c. whole wheat flour
1 1/4 c. warm water
1/4 c. buttermilk
1 T. yeast
1 t. sea salt

Mix 2 cups of the flour and all other ingredients well, about 3 minutes by hand. Then gradually add another 1 1/2 - 2 cups flour to make a stiff dough and knead this for 10 min. Cover and let rise about 45 minutes in a warm place (if you are in a hurry, omit this step). Place on a floured surface and shape into a log, about 2" in diameter. Cut the log into 1 1/2" slices. Shape into balls and roll from center out to edges to form circles about 7-8" in diameter. Place on preheated baking sheet on the middle shelf of a 500° F oven for 4-6 minutes, or until pita puffs up and browns slightly. Remove from oven and cover with a towel until cool, then store in a plastic bag in fridge or freezer.

QUICK SKILLET BREAD

A simple gluten-free bread, great for breakfast or anytime. This bread is much like a flatbread and can be garnished with sesame seeds, poppy seeds, toasted flax seeds, or sunflower seeds.

2/3 cup water, room temperature
1/2 cup garbanzo bean flour
2 t. extra virgin olive oil
1/16 t. sea salt

Preheat a 12-inch, nonstick sauté pan.* Whisk the flour, salt and water together. Batter will be thin. When a drop of water sizzles on the sauté pan, add 1 teaspoon oil and tilt the pan to coat. Pour batter into the pan all at once (as if making a giant crepe). Tilt pan to distribute evenly. Cover and cook over medium-high heat 2 minutes. Drizzle remaining oil over the bread. Spread with back of spoon to lightly coat top surface. Cook 5 more minutes, uncovered. When edges of bread appear dry, turn over. Reduce heat to medium-low. Cook 5 more minutes, uncovered. Remove to wire rack. Serve warm.

*If you don't have a 12" sauté pan, prepare half a recipe and cook in an 8-10" pan. Keep bread warm while you cook the next one.

CORNTILLAS

1 c. fine corn flour
1 c. water
2 t. whole wheat flour
2 t. lime juice
1 t. Mrs. Dash® Table Blend Seasoning
1 t. sea salt
1/2 t. onion powder
1/4 t. each of garlic powder and black pepper

Mix well, and drop by tablespoon onto lightly oiled baking sheet. Spread into circles with back of spoon to about 4-5 inches across. Mixture should be fairly thick, but spread evenly, so the corntilla will bake evenly. Bake at 350° F for 8 minutes, then turn over and cook for 5 more minutes. Makes about 12 corntillas.

Variation: **Crispy Corn Chips** - spread mixture a little thinner and cook for 9-10 minutes, or until crisp. If eaten with a salty dip or filling, reduce salt to 1/2 t.

RICE WRAPS

The pea, rice, and corn flours in these wraps form a complete protein.

2/3 c. water
3 T. brown rice flour
3 T. corn meal
2 T. green pea flour
1/8 t. sea salt or to taste

Whisk all ingredients together. Lightly spray 10-12" non-stick crepe or sauté pan with oil. Place over medium-high heat. When hot, (drop of water will sizzle), pour batter into pan and tilt to spread evenly. (If using a smaller pan, use only part of the batter.) Cover and cook 2 minutes. Spray batter lightly with oil, and cook 5 more minutes, uncovered. When edges of wrap appear dry, turn over. Reduce heat to medium-low and cook another 4-5 minutes. Makes one large wrap. Serve warm. To double the recipe, use 1/3 c. of each flour, 1 1/3 c. water and 1/4 t. salt.

Variations: 1/4 c. brown rice flour and 1/4 c. corn flour
1/4 c. garbanzo flour and 1/4 c. corn flour
1/4 c. garbanzo flour and 1/4 c. brown rice flour

WHOLE WHEAT FLATBREAD

2 c. whole wheat flour
2 t. baking powder
1/2 t. sea salt
3/4 c. water, or enough to make a stiff dough

Combine dry ingredients, and then add water gradually. Knead dough
(by hand or with electric bread mixer) until elastic, about 10-15 minutes
by hand, or 4-6 minutes in mixer. Take about 1/3 cup of dough and roll
with a rolling pin until it is 4-5 inches in diameter.

Place on a cast iron or other heavy skillet (do not use oil) and cook over
medium to medium high heat until lightly browned on both sides.

These flatbreads can be eaten plain, topped with cheese or with Mrs.
Dash® seasonings (we like *Classic Italiano* and *Minced Onion Medley*); as a
wrap, filled with your favorite vegetables (peppers, cucumbers, tomatoes, lettuce, etc.); or drizzled with Ranch or Italian dressing. Makes 6
flatbreads.

Variations:
Seasoned Flatbread Make flatbread dough. Roll out to individual
sizes, and sprinkle with Mrs. Dash® or McCormick's Season All®. Roll
over the seasoning with a rolling pin to press into dough, then cook
until lightly brown both sides.

South of the Border Flatbread Add 2 t. chopped cilantro to uncooked
flatbread, and roll over it once with a rolling pin. Lightly brown both
sides and spread with your favorite salsa. Sprinkle one side lightly
with mozzarella cheese. Put back in skillet and cover with pan lid.
Cook 2-3 minutes on medium heat to melt the cheese.

Spread *Rita's Famous 5-Minute Bean Dip* (p. 86) over flatbread and top
with cheese or cottage cheese, if desired.

COLORFUL VEGGIE FLATBREAD

Green:
1 recipe Whole Wheat Flatbread
1/4 c. chopped parsley

Follow regular flatbread directions.

Orange:
1 recipe Whole Wheat Flatbread
1/4 c. chopped red pepper (fresh or canned)

Follow regular flatbread directions. Knead in extra flour if necessary.

RYE WRAPS

1 1/2 T. yeast
1 1/4 c. warm water
3 1/2-4 c. light rye flour
1 T. caraway seeds
1 t. sea salt
1/4 c. applesauce
1 1/2 t. honey

Soften yeast in 1/4 cup of the warm water and let rise until doubled. In separate mixing bowl, combine dry ingredients, reserving 1/2 cup of the rye flour. Make a nest in the center of dry ingredients and stir in remaining ingredients, adding the yeast mixture last. Mix well, adding reserved flour as needed. Turn dough out onto floured surface and knead until dough feels smooth and is no longer sticky, adding additional flour if necessary. Divide dough into golf ball-sized portions. Preheat oven and a lightly sprayed baking sheet to 500° F. Roll each portion out very thin, like a tortilla. Place wraps on the preheated baking sheet. Cook for 1 1/2 minutes on each side, or until lightly toasted.

Place hot wraps in a gallon zip-top bag, or cover with plastic wrap to keep from drying out. Wraps will be a bit stiff, so fill them generously so they can be rolled up without cracking.

For pizza crust, roll dough 1/8" thick, and cook a few minutes longer.

INDEX

All Things Cool

B'Nana-Nut Squares 30
Banana Cashew Cream 40
Banana Freezies 29
Banana Maple Smoothie 22
Banana Popsicles 23
Banana-Ade 22
Berry Tasty "Drinky Drink" 26
Blueberry Boost 24
Blueberry Cashew Cream 38
"Brown Sugar" Banana
  Cashew Cream 40
Chilly Haystacks 30
Choco-'Nana-Nut Pops 31
Chocolate Cashew Cream 37
Chocolate Dipping Sauce
  for Banana Freezies 30
Chocolate Ice Cream 34
Chocolate Mint Cashew Cream 37
Chocolate Mint Pops 32
Choco-Peanut Cashew Cream 39
Citrus Mint Popsicles 31
Clair's Favorite Strawberry
  Cashew Cream 38
Coco-Mango-'Nana Sherbet 36
Coconut Cashew Cream 39
Double Chocolate Nut
  Cashew Cream 37
Emilee's Banana Freeze 23
Flavored Waters 28
Frozen Fruit 29
Honey Soy Nog 27
"Just Peachy" Sherbet 36
Lemon Grape Pops 31
Lemon Grapeade 28
Lemon Sherbet 35
Mango Ice Cream 33
Maple Nut Cashew Cream 40
Nutty Chocolate Ice Cream 34
Orange Crème Pops 32
Peach Dream 23
Peanut Butter-Banana
  Cashew Cream 38
Pumpkin Pie Coolers 32
Raspberry Cashew Cream 37
Raspberry Chip Cashew Cream 37
Raspberry Mango Ice Cream 33
Raspberry-Mint Flavored Water 29
Raz-a-Mango Smoothie 24
Raz-a-Nana Smoothie 25
Shannon's "Drinky Drink" 25
Soy Egg Nog 27
Soy Nog 27
Soy-Orange Julius 25
Soy-Orange Sherbet 36
Strawberry Mint Breeze 26
Strawberry Punch 26
Tropical Treat Smoothie 24
Tropical Trio Sherbet 35
Vanilla Nut Cashew Cream 39
Vanilla Nut Shake 22
Very Berry Banana Smoothie 23
Watermelon Ice Cream 34
Watermelon Sorbet 39

Candies

Almond Butter Toffee 48
Berry Candy 42
Carob Chippers 45
Chocolate Logs 44
Chocolate Mint Honey Candy 45
Clair's Favorite Date
  Pecan Brittle 46
Cocoa Nut Fudge 45
Honey Candy 42
Honey Caramels 43
Lemon Candy 42
Marshmallow Squares 47
Molasses Caramels 44
Molasses Taffy 44
Nut 'n Honey Candy 42
Nut Rolls 43
Orange Candy 42
Peanut Butter and Jelly
  Barber Poles 43
Peanut Butter Candy 42
Peanut Butter Toffee 48
Peanut Marshmallow Squares 48
Pink Peppermint Candy 42
Pistachio Honey Squares 46
Sesame Honey Candy 46

Cookies, Bars, and Muffins

Almond Chocolate Chip Bars 65
Almond Date Sugarplums 60
Apple-Date Fiber Bars 66
Apricot Bars 61
Banana Nut Muffins 70
Berry Good No-Bakes 51
Blender Brownies 67
Blondie Bites 62
Brownie Bites 62
Cashew, Date and Raisin Bars 64
Choco-Date Fiber Bars 66
Chocolate Cashew Date Bars 63
Chocolate Peanut Butter Balls 56
Chocolate Raisin Balls 56
Chocolate Raisin Cashew Bites 61

Index

Choco-Malted Brownie Bars 63
Cinnamon Crunch Muffins 70
Coconut Macaroons...........................57
Coconut No-Bakes 51
Cole's Double Nut Date Bars............63
Daily Energy Bars 64
Date and Nut No-Bakes.....................51
Excellent Oatmeal Chocolate
     Chip Cookies................................54
Ginni's Gingersnaps...........................55
Health Nut Cookies 53
Honey Krispies...................................50
Honey No-Bake Cookies....................51
Jam Thumbprint Cookies...................51
Jumble Cookies...................................56
Katon's Almond Bites 65
Kelsey's Pistachio Bites.....................65
Lemon Bars 67
Multi-Grain Muffins 69
No-Bake Chocolate Cookies..............50
Nutty Raspberry Brownie Bites........62
Oat and Barley Bars 68
Old Fashioned Oatmeal
     Cookies..57
Omega 3 Bars.....................................61
One and One-Half Cookies 62
One and One-Half Raisin
     Nut Cookies.................................62
PB&J No-Bakes 52
Peanut Butter Banana Muffins..........69
Peanut Butter Chocolate Bites...........60
Peanut Butter Cookies........................54
Peanut Butter Raspberry Bites 54
Plum Delicious Peanut Butter
     Bites 65
Pumpkin Chocolate Chip
     Cookies..55
Pumpkin Cookies................................55
Raisin No-Bakes 51
Raspberry Oat Bars............................68
Saucepan Cookies 52
Snowy Peanut Butter Cookies...........54
Triple Treat Sugarplums 60
Sweet Multi-Grain Muffins 69
Vanilla Peanut Bars 60
Walnut Raisin Sugarplums................59

Crispy Crunchies

Alphabet Vegetables 72
Apple Cinnamon Crackers.................80
Apple Cinnamon Trail Mix 79
Barbecue Crackers..............................73
Basic Crackers....................................73
Chili Crackers 74

Chili Lime Cashews............................76
Cinnamon-Sucanat Wedges...............78
Crispy Potato Wedges 72
Crunchy Almond Snacks 78
Garlic and Onion Cashews.................76
Garlic Italian Crackers........................73
Ginger Masala Cashews.....................76
Honeyed Cashews 78
Nutty Popcorn 80
Oriental Wheat and Seed Mix............75
Popped Wheat and Seeds 74
Roasted Black Pepper Cashews 75
Roasted Nuts and Seeds 75
Salsa Crackers....................................73
Sucanuts 77
Sugar Corn 80
Taco Nuts..77
Taco Seasoning Mix 77
Trail Mix 79

Dips

Bingham's Fresh Salsa 85
Buttermilk Ranch Dip 83
Citrus Fruit Dip..................................87
Cool Cucumber Dip............................84
Creamy Chive Dip 83
Cucumber Guacamole.........................85
Cucumber-Yogurt Dip........................84
Easy Hummus and Red
     Pepper Dip...................................82
Fruit Salsa..88
Green Olive Hummus Dip 82
Original Hummus Dip........................82
Peanut Butter Yogurt Dip 87
Piña Colada Dip.................................88
Quick 'N Easy Bean Dip 85
Red Raspberry Fruit Dip....................87
Rita's Famous 5-Minute
     Bean Dip.......................................86
Spicy Hot Dip 83
Strawberry Dip 87
Sweet Mint Dip..................................88
Thousand Island Dip..........................83
Tomato Basil Dip................................84

Snack Wraps

Colorful Veggie Flatbread..................93
Corntillas 91
Crispy Corn Chips 91
Pita Pockets 90
Quick Skillet Bread 90
Rice Wraps 91
Rye Wraps 93
Whole Wheat Flatbread 92

NATURAL MEALS PUBLISHING
1-888-232-6706

www.naturalmeals.com   E-mail: order@naturalmeals.com

COUNTRY BEANS *by Rita Bingham*
Nearly 400 quick, easy meatless bean recipes with over 110 bean flour recipes, including FAST, fat-free 3 minute bean soups and 5-minute bean dips. Most recipes are wheat free, gluten free, and dairy-free. Recipes guaranteed to change the way you use beans! **$14.95**

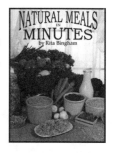

NATURAL MEALS IN MINUTES *by Rita Bingham*
Over 300 quick, high in fiber, low in fat, meatless recipes using basic foods: whole grains, legumes, vegetables, fruits, sprouts, and 3-minute fat-free powdered milk cheeses. Each recipe lists nutritional information. Learn sneaky tips on adding extra fiber to every meal! **$14.95**

1-2-3 SMOOTHIES *by Rita Bingham*
123 quick and frosty drinks - they are delicious AND nutritious! These energy boosting drinks are the best healthy treats ever! 100% natural ingredients - no sugar, preservatives, or artificial sweeteners. **$14.95**

FOOD COMBINING *by Rita Bingham*
Better health, the *natural* way. Take charge of your health. Learn how to combine the best foods on earth (fruits, vegetables, grains, legumes, nuts, and seeds) for best digestion, increased energy, and *improved* health. **$7.95**